HYPNOSIS:
The Mind/Body Connection

HYPNOSIS:
The Mind/Body Connection

*Discover Your Infinite Potential
for Self-Healing and Growth*

PETER H. C. MUTKE, M.D.

WESTWOOD PUBLISHING COMPANY, INC.
700 South Central Ave., Glendale, CA 91203
818-242-1159

For Reorder or for a FREE CATALOG:
WESTWOOD PUBLISHING CO.
700 S. Central Ave.
Glendale, CA 91203
(818) 242-1159
FAX: (818) 247-9379

Formerly titled: Selective Awareness

ISBN 0-930298-71-3
87 88 89 90   10 9 8 7 6 5 4 3 2 1

Printed in the United States of America

Acknowledgments

I wish to thank my patients who presented a never-ending source of information and whose cooperation led to the development of Selective Awareness Therapy. This undertaking would not have been possible without the solid foundation I gained from my teachers throughout my medical education.

I wish to thank my colleagues of the medical societies of Monterey County and Marin County for their support and compassion, watching my development without judgment.

I am grateful to the John F. Kennedy University and especially to its students for their interest and help in my teaching of this new form of therapy.

Among the many who have contributed to this work, one person stands out through her persistent and kind encouragement that led to the publishing of this book — Dr. Virginia Satir.

About the Author

As the father of Selective Awareness Therapy, Dr. Peter Mutke is internationally renowned for furthering the understanding of the mind/body interaction in curing diseases and other dysfunctions. A cum laude graduate from Heidelberg University, Germany, in medicine, Dr. Mutke did his internship and residency in California, where he practiced surgery.

Dissatisfied with the lack of answers as to why people become ill, Dr. Mutke continued his studies in psychology and began to specialize in psychotherapy and psychomatic medicine. He then studied acupuncture and did research in Biofeedback.

Dr. Mutke has taught in the United States at the John F. Kennedy University in Orinda, California, and at the University of California, Berkeley. He is currently lecturing throughout Europe and teaching in Berlin, Germany.

Contents

Foreword

Today is a time of miracles. Look at what is happening to "modern man" in "modern society": He is going to the moon, learning the secrets of the atom, and experiencing an explosion in the science of genetics. These revolutions are fast changing the way we look at life around us.

There is also a much greater miracle going on now which is revolutionizing our ideas about health — namely, the capacity of the human being to heal his own body. What was previously thought to be old wives' tales or the result of magic or simply coincidence is now emerging as something more real, a phenomenon supported by scientific data, biofeedback, biorhythm, Kirlian photography, and thermography — all of which have opened up new possibilities for the physical and spiritual benefit of mankind.

Peter Mutke has built on these new knowledges. *Selective Awareness* shows in a step-by-step, understandable procedure how to make contact with and between our various human parts in order to attain greater control over our health. Benjamin Franklin did not invent electricity, he only discovered it. I think it is the same way with the kinds of forces and energy that Peter Mutke describes in this book.

Medicine is the science directed toward healing the physical body. "Good medicine" is dependent upon one person, the doctor, doing something to someone else, the patient, often without the patient's understanding of what is happening to him or how he might participate and assist in his own healing.

Peter Mutke, a physician with substantial medical experience, repeatedly encountered serious limits to his abilities to effect healing. The scientist and the human in him urged him to study further the whole matter of healing. He left his practice in order to free his time to study different forms of healing throughout the world. Out of these experiences came a sense of excitement and the possibility of a new healing dimension that assists the patient in identifying and using his own healing resources. *Selective Awareness* simply and clearly sets forth Mutke's findings, enabling the reader to put them to immediate use.

We stand at the threshold of a radically new world in which the individual can manage his own health. Through this valuable guide, Peter Mutke has made a substantial contribution to the practice of self-healing.

Virginia Satir

Introduction

This book is designed to help you improve your health and change your outlook on life. It presumes that you want to function at your highest physical and psychological levels, that you want to improve your health and will practice getting well.

To take full advantage of all Selective Awareness Therapy can offer, you must give yourself the cooperation necessary to establish discipline as you work on your goals and the compassion to allow enough time to accomplish them. When you are able to concentrate on yourself and on the internal mechanisms that keep you functioning well, you will find that change occurs rather quickly. The greater your self-understanding, the greater your ability to mobilize your self-corrective potential toward health.

Selective Awareness presents not only information about health and illness but also step-by-step exercises to effect health changes based on an understanding of your own physical and psychological processes. When you do these exercises you will find an immediate improvement in your physical and mental health.

Some of the benefits you will gain from these exercises in Selective Awareness are:

Relaxation
Increased awareness of self
Increased ability and desire to change
Control over the autonomic functions of your body.

In addition to a sense of enthusiasm and adventure, you will need to contribute the following:

Cooperation
Concentration
Imagination
Understanding
Compassion
Motivation.

(You will also need a notebook to carry out the exercises and a tape recorder to facilitate your initial work in Selective Awareness.)

Your Benefits

Relaxation

While you are in a state of Selective Awareness during these exercises, your brain wave pattern changes to the tranquil alpha range, the altered state of consciousness attained in meditation or in biofeedback by those who have been properly trained. This shift is in itself therapeutic, allowing you to discharge the tensions that have built up during the day. The accompanying reduction of muscular tensions leaves you refreshed and reduces or relieves symptoms caused by tension. You may notice this improvement as soon as you have finished the exercise.

Increased Awareness

In the state of Selective Awareness, you will have access to information about the physical and mental causes that have allowed ill health to prevail. These may be psychological, such as poor self-image or expectation of sickness, or physical symptoms like ulcers or headaches. Selective Awareness will help you to know where and how to make beneficial adjustments.

Increased Ability and Desire to Change

How often do we say, "Tomorrow I'm going on a diet," or "I'll quit smoking on my birthday," or "I'm determined to get to the office on time Monday." We all know what we would like to change about ourselves. The exercises in Selective Awareness Therapy will help you do more than talk about it — they will help you produce change. All you need to do is to believe in your own power and practice the exercises with confidence that *you are* capable of altering your lifestyle, habits, and malfunctions.

Control of Autonomic Functions

You will notice that in Selective Awareness you have great influence over the functions of your autonomic nervous systems. You will learn to control your blood pressure, adjust organ function, and enhance the dynamics of healing to the point where you can actually learn to control blood flow and bleeding. By learning to understand your internal language, you can use Selective Awareness techniques for regulatory change without the need for expensive and complicated biofeedback equipment. The body frequently misallocates energy, expending too much on one symptom or area of the body — on negative preoccupations of the mind — thus robbing other areas. When this happens, healing can't take place, and you can't get well. Using Selective Awareness techniques, you can learn to break up these energy blocks and to reroute the liberated energy to where it's needed for healing.

Your Contribution

What you need to contribute to make your own experience of Selective Awareness meaningful are the following:

Cooperation

To benefit from Selective Awareness you must take yourself seriously and establish a regular rhythm of reading this book and doing the exercises described. The sense of accomplishment you will get from this discipline is a positive change in itself. In fact, the wish to change, expressed in a state of Selective Awareness, is already a big step toward that change. This is what is meant by "increased ability and desire to change."

Concentration

Do not merely glance through this book. It is an action book that requires you to concentrate on yourself, on the feelings and physical processes within your mind-body system. Make room for concentrated work on a daily basis. Once you have mastered Selective Awareness Therapy you can practice it wherever and whenever you choose. Many people who have been working with Selective Awareness for some time take a few minutes a day to practice the techniques in their offices or at home. As with any discipline, however, you must be willing to take the time and do the work necessary at the beginning. Soon you will notice positive change.

Imagination

Throughout this book you will be asked to rehearse healthful images, or images of the achievement of a desired result. Your daily life is consistent with your self-image. If your self-image of health is brittle, so may be your actual health. When you learn the ability to create positive images of yourself, you will notice positive changes within your mind-body health concept as your self-image becomes strong and healthy.

Understanding

The better you understand the dynamic interaction between mind and body, the more sensibly you will be able to make positive, long-lasting adjustments. You will be given techniques for understanding the actual mechanics of the mind-body interaction and methods of checking the information you receive. With this understanding, you can take your health into your own hands or augment an already-existing health program.

Compassion

Give yourself a break. Learn how to avoid getting angry at yourself when you are depressed, when things don't work out, or when you have an illness that lingers on. Give yourself the compassion to learn from your own experience, whether of illness or of health.

Motivation

In part, the benefits you can receive from Selective Awareness depend on the strength of your motivation. If you have spent a great deal of money on sickness, are living day by day on numerous prescriptions, or face the possibility of surgery, you will be highly motivated to make Selective Awareness a new health concept for yourself. As you practice the exercises in this book you will support your own self-corrective potential toward physical and mental health. You will find that mind-body integration toward health is not limited to times of ill health but is designed for health maintenance as well.

One

Selective Awareness Therapy

What Is Selective Awareness?

Selective Awareness is a tool that you can use to achieve harmony of mind and body. Selective Awareness is a state of mind. In fact, you are in a state of Selective Awareness right now. Sit quietly for a moment and just listen. Concentrate all your awareness on your ears and on the sounds that are pouring into them. What do you hear? Traffic in the street? An airplane overhead? Children playing outside? Perhaps there is a leaky faucet dripping in the kitchen or a clock ticking quietly in the same room. If it were very quiet outside, you could actually hear the sound of your blood circulating in your body. But you have been aware of none of these sounds — you have automatically screened them out so that you could concentrate on the task of reading this book.

Now imagine that you hear the telephone ringing, faintly, in another part of the house. You will probably hear this sound and respond to it, even though it's no louder than many of the sounds you've been screening out. You have unconsciously selected a state of awareness that will filter out sounds you don't need to know about and let in sounds that carry important information, such as the ringing of the telephone.

If you were not in a state of Selective Awareness, you would not be able to concentrate on any one thing because every bit of stimulus that reached you would be equally important and equally demanding of your attention.

What Is Selective Awareness Therapy?

Selective Awareness Therapy uses the principle of Selective Awareness to allow you to focus your concentration on areas of physical and mental imbalance, to understand the symptoms of ill health, and to release healing energy wherever it is needed. It is a tool for the integration of mind and body. One basic assumption of Selective Awareness Therapy is that you are born with a self-corrective potential toward health and that ill health occurs when the harmonious balance of mind and body is upset. This continual process of self-regulation, or balance, is called *homeostasis*, and its job is to see that, after times of stress or injury, the body will return to normal functioning after healing has taken place. If a symptom continues to linger after its usefulness has ended, that's a sign that the mind and body are no longer working together harmoniously and that energy is being misallocated.

Selective Awareness is experienced as a letting go, a relaxation that is both physical and mental. And in that state of peace you are able to get in touch with those avenues of thought and feeling that lead to homeostasis. With this increased understanding, you will be able to change toward homeostasis, health, and the harmony of mind and body working together.

Another underlying assumption of Selective Awareness Therapy is that both physical and psychological symptoms are the products of unresolved thought-emotion complexes that upset your homeostatic balance by misallocating energy. This misallocation of energy may actually cause illness. This means that how you think and what you feel influence your physical health. The reverse is also true: If you have a physical symptom for very long, it will change the way you think and feel about everything else (the thought-emotion complex).

Misallocation of Energy Causes Illness

An example of how this misallocation of energy causes illness is the case of Pam, who was referred by a colleague of mine who also believes in a holistic approach to medicine. (Holism is the belief that entities, such as individual human beings or other organisms or organ systems, function as complete units that cannot be reduced to their individual parts. Holistic medicine is more interested in unifying than in classifying, and it takes into consideration the interaction of mind, body, and environment rather than just an isolated symptom or disease process.)

Pam was referred to me because of persistent pain in the lower back following two operations and lengthy hospitalization. I saw her for four visits and taught her to use Selective Awareness Therapy. Several months later I received the following letter, which she was kind enough to let me reproduce.

> Dear Dr. Mutke:
> Although I couldn't understand or admit it at the time, I now realize what a mess I was in when my doctor referred me to you. Having sustained a severe back injury two years before, survived two subsequent surgeries, and spent one hundred, forty-one days in the hospital as well as the better part of two years in bed, I still had horrendous pain that prevented me from walking and, in fact, kept me flat on my back. This caused severe depression to the point where, even though I didn't want to die, I surely didn't want to live that way. I was, as you know, averse to coming to you, but when you assured me that you weren't going to hypnotize me I agreed to try it. That was the most positive and advantageous decision I ever made!
>
> During our first session, I learned that when extreme pain such as I was suffering is that prolonged, it is possible that something of which I am totally unaware could be interfering with the healing process. Once I accepted this premise and knew also that my pain was legitimate, my therapy was a breeze!
>
> Through my conversations with you and your putting me into the welcomed "state of Selective Awareness," I not only experienced the most relaxed state I've ever known, but I became acutely aware of influences that had

apparently been buried in my subconscious mind for a long time. I must have talked your ear off, for believe me, the garbage really came out that day!

In the following three sessions I came to grips with two realities: first, that subconsciously I was harboring an abundance of fear, anxiety, anger, frustration, and resentment regarding my back. Reviewing what I had been through I could certainly understand why. Then I had to accept that I was experiencing many of the same emotions in my marriage. Once I was able to unload these hitherto unknown burdens I felt higher than a kite! Through the state of Selective Awareness and by reviewing my illness and my marriage, I learned that there were psychological factors which were preventing my healing and manifesting themselves in severe physical pain. WOW! What a revelation! When I realized what influence my mind could have over my body and what, in turn, I could do about it, I wanted to run out into the street, stop the traffic, and shout, "Hey, look at me and what I learned to do!!"

Needless to say, my pain wasn't gone after only four visits. As you said, that would be magic. But, I threw away my crutches, returned to being the positive person I once was, and started living again! I continued listening to my tapes every day which helped me to relax so the pain gradually decreased, and with your counseling, my husband and I were able to resolve our difficulties and now have a beautiful relationship.

I am swimming often and hike six to eight miles every week and I still am subjected to the discomfort of sore muscles. But that's OK and I can accept it and live with it. But I am proud of the fact that I have taken no muscle relaxers or pain medication since our first session six months ago!

I am well, I am happy, and I am confident that I can handle the situation should it arise again. So many positive results have come from my therapy. Would you think me crazy if I told you that I'm glad it all happened?

My husband once called you his wife's miracle doctor. You replied that you didn't work the miracle, I did. Well, maybe so, but my sincere thanks to you for giving me the tools to do so!

Gratefully,
Pam

It frequently happens that when a person returns to health through Selective Awareness Therapy, other problems in his or her life straighten themselves out quite naturally. In Pam's case, the adjustment toward homeostasis actually produced a new clinical picture. She came in with complaints of insomnia and hand tremor, and in evaluating her, I came to the conclusion that she was suffering from an overactive thyroid. When I proposed that to her, she said, "Oh, I am taking thyroid medication and have been taking it for 17 years." As Pam's whole body-mind system returned to homeostasis, so did her thyroid gland, and the medication that she had been taking for her underactive thyroid now gave her symptoms of excess, which promptly subsided when she discontinued the medication.

In this case, Pam had been directing a great deal of negative emotional energy to the area of her lower back. All of the fear, anger, and resentment that she experienced, including her feelings about her marriage, went straight to her back and were manifested as physical symptoms.

Linking the Symptom and the Thought-Emotion

Any symptom — a headache, for example, or smoking too much, or overeating — is a reflection of a *thought-emotion complex* that an individual has not properly "digested" and that is contrary to his values, assumptions, and expectations. The symptom, then, is an expression of the unresolved thought-emotion process. Most thought-emotion complexes of a severe nature have a physical-psychological component. The goal of Selective Awareness Therapy is to make a link between the physical symptom, or the psychological symptom, and the thought-emotion process of which it is a reflection or breakthrough.

How a situation is perceived is more important than the factual data of that situation. When an individual interprets a situation and forms an assumption, that assumption continues to operate without his conscious knowledge. This process is especially significant during the earliest period of life about which the adult has no conscious memory. When the infant perceives a situation on a primitive level, without critical reasoning, his perceptions become assumptions that take on a symbolic significance. These assumptions will govern his responses to future situations, even though they are completely unconscious. How these faulty assumptions may be adjusted through Selective Awareness Therapy is illustrated in the following case history.

Changing Your Faulty Assumptions

Lisa, a young college student, complained of a tremendous emotional distance between her father and herself, for which neither knew the cause. In Selective Awareness Therapy she recalled an incident that took place when she was only one year old. "I am lying in my crib and my father is trying to suffocate me."

Traumatized by this incident, she assumed that her father was trying to kill her. That was a fact — her fact. She was not aware that her unconscious mind had made this assumption. Each time her father tried to be affectionate and intimate, she unconsciously assumed, "He's trying to do me in again." Therefore, every interaction with her father documented the validity of this primitive assumption.

Further exploration in Selective Awareness revealed that, in actuality, the father had returned home late from work to be greeted by an exhausted wife and a screaming daughter. He had tried to quiet his daughter's crying by putting his hand over her mouth and gently saying, "Shh."

From the information gained in recalling this incident, Lisa realized not only that her assumption about her father was incorrect but that it had prevented her from establishing a close relationship with him. She could now view her infantile reaction as a symbolic expression of irrational fear of her father.

In correcting this early assumption, Lisa could see how she had manipulated her father's responses to further validate it. Finally, she was able to establish a new relationship with her father based on the loving care that had, in fact, always been present.

Lisa's case history illustrates the "Law of Sensitization," which states that a sensitized person will distort incoming messages to confirm the validity of the sensitization. Because of her early trauma, Lisa translated all messages from her father into threats in order to validate her belief that he was trying to harm her. Through Selective Awareness Therapy she was able to reassess her early assumptions and to change them in the direction of health.

Therapy means change, and the increased receptivity to change is one of the benefits of Selective Awareness Therapy. The responsibility for change is yours. You are the one who is changing, you are the one who knows how you want to change. Selective Awareness Therapy can serve as a catalyst for change, and it can show you how to make your change effective.

How Does Selective Awareness Therapy Work?

After you have become familiar with Selective Awareness and its inductions, you will begin your therapy by focusing on a pleasant, relaxing image. Focusing means concentrating all your attention in one direction and screening out unnecessary noises and distractions, including the stray thoughts that frequently pop up when you are trying to concentrate. Then you will learn to focus your attention on a past event that is related to the symptom you are working on — a "symptom-producing event." By reviewing the event in a state of Selective Awareness, you will be able to learn important information about it — "What emotion is produced by this event? How do I feel?" This is important information because the energy that is tied up in the symptom can be released through understanding the thought-emotion content that goes with it — and, once released, that energy can be used for healing.

After you have reviewed three or four symptom-producing events, you will understand the emotional content of your headache, your overeating, or whatever other symptom you are working on.

There are many tools you can use in Selective Awareness to get at the thought-emotion content of the symptom-producing event. One of these is *ideomotor finger signals*, signals from yourself to yourself that let you know when you are on the path to mind-body harmony.

Another of these tools is *image rehearsal*, a process for encouraging your mind to accept the new and positive image of yourself that you choose.

Your *self-image* plays an important part in the state of your health. An injured self-image may be allowing you to accept a state of imbalance as normal. Selective Awareness Therapy gives you exercises to raise your self-image, particularly your image of your own health.

Since you are the creator of your own self-image, and you are the only one capable of changing it, you must ask for and receive your own permission to change, every step of the way. The system of CONSIDER, CONSULT, CONSENT is basic and most important to Selective Awareness Therapy. "Is it OK to give up these headaches? Is it all right to consider not smoking? Would it be OK to be twenty pounds lighter?" This system for checking your progress and understanding your internal messages every step of the way allows you to be uniquely involved in your own therapy.

Another important technique of Selective Awareness Therapy is *age regression*, an "unlocking device" for the vault of treasures and traumas of childhood. With age regression, you will learn to go back to a specific time, take a look around, find out for yourself what is going on. Where are you? How old are you? What do you feel? This technique makes it possible for you to reach and understand feelings and emotions that would otherwise be difficult to get to.

These techniques, and others, will be fully explained when you begin to practice Selective Awareness Therapy.

Finding Symptom-Producing Events

The following case history illustrates how Selective Awareness Therapy is used to orient back to symptom-producing events and to eliminate their negative influence on adult life.

Louis was a 45-year-old businessman who was referred to me with a ten-year history of severe stomach problems — hyperacidity with gastritis and muscle spasms, as well as peptic ulcers. Louis' own written evaluation of himself included the following comments. "I am a nervous person. I can't seem to unwind. I am highly perfectionistic and uptight, and it all reflects in my stomach. I have constant constipation, gastritis, and acid stomach. I toss and turn all night with pain."

Louis wrote several pages about his current life situation which showed him to be hyperactive in his business life, constantly striving for greater success. He was vice president in charge of sales for a large company, with a staff of over 100 in his department, and very much concerned with being the best — the best businessman, the best boss, and the best provider for his family. He was strongly motivated to make a lot of money, believing that to be the most important role of a successful husband and father.

As the first step in Louis' Selective Awareness Therapy, I described the dynamics of health and illness in relation to the thought-emotion-physical symptom process. He was very interested in the idea of self-healing and soon had a good understanding of how his emotional problems were reflected in his stomach and digestive tract.

In the state of Selective Awareness, Louis oriented back to his most recent symptom-producing event and saw himself rushing around his office doing six things at once, feeling harassed, driven, and frustrated — and experiencing great pain in his stomach. Orienting back to other times when his symptoms were especially severe, he saw himself a few weeks earlier, experiencing great anger in dealing with a particularly difficult customer. Then back to his college years, trying to support himself through school by selling encyclopedias, feeling great frustration because there's only so much he can do, and he has no time to study. And finally, as a ten-year-old newsboy, winning his parents' approval by selling more and more papers.

The common threads running through these symptom-producing events were frustration and anger at never being able to do enough, and a feeling of being driven to do more and more.

At the end of this first session, Louis made himself a relaxation tape recording that stressed the possibility of enjoying life moment by moment, without the need to rush on to the next activity before completing the task at hand. He continued his Selective Awareness Therapy at home, making several more tapes for himself. His personal history notebook for this period shows a dramatic alleviation of symptoms. He was able to sleep soundly and didn't have to take any medication for pain.

After about three weeks, however, his stomach problems began to return, and he found himself speeding up again, rushing from task to task, feeling that old anger and frustration building up. He called me for a second appointment, and this time his wife Ellen came with him. Louis had neglected to mention that he and his wife were having marital difficulties, and that in the past, as now, when his stomach improved his marriage got worse. It seems that Louis' stomach was reflecting not only his own frustration and anger, but his wife's as well.

Selective Awareness exploration showed that for years Ellen had felt neglected by her husband and jealous of his seeming preference for his job. But both had become so accustomed to the situation that when Louis' physical and emotional state began to improve, their relationship, which had been delicately balanced, began to deteriorate.

Ellen and Louis continued their Selective Awareness Therapy together at home, exploring the symptom-producing events in their marriage and their home life. They were very inventive in making tapes for themselves and for each other. This mutual recognition allowed them to regain the harmony of their early days together, and Louis' stomach problems improved dramatically at the same time. The resulting shift in values away from the business world and toward the home also improved Louis' relationship with his children, who had seen him as something of a bad-tempered stranger.

But the change that Louis seemed proudest of was that he stopped biting his fingernails. For the first time in his life, he was able to have a manicure.

My Evolution of Selective Awareness Therapy

Throughout my career as a medical doctor and surgeon I have been continually amazed at how differently people react to illness. Some patients are cured as though by magic, while in others illness hangs on and on — or rather it seems that the patient is hanging on to the illness! In the 1920s the psychologist Emile Coué recommended that his patients use the formula, "Every day in every way I am getting better and better." But it seems that many people, particularly those with persistent health problems, have adopted the opposite formula: "Every day in every way I am getting worse and worse."

While I was puzzling over how quickly and easily some people are able to recover from devastating illness or surgery, I attended a clinical demonstration of hypnosis by Milton Erickson, M.D., the brilliant therapist and author in the field of therapeutic hypnosis. I came away from that demonstration excited and even more curious about the possibility of conscious control over body functions.

Then I was presented with a dramatic example of the power of hypnosis. My wife and I were on vacation in an isolated ski resort. One evening she complained of nausea and mild pain; by midnight she was vomiting and had acute pain in her back. Then she told me that she had been passing blood in her urine since early afternoon.

I almost panicked as the bleeding grew severe and I realized that she was bleeding from her kidneys. The last train had left the resort and the roads were snowed in. There was nothing I could do except try to make her more comfortable. Suddenly I remembered the hospital demonstration of hypnosis, in which the patient had been instructed to control bleeding. In fact, I did more than remember it — I *saw* the whole thing and was able to review the steps that I should take in this emergency.

I induced a hypnotic trance in my wife, gave her the proper suggestions for the contraction of the blood vessels that were causing the bleeding, and within a few minutes, the nausea, pain, and bleeding had stopped and she was asleep. It was a long time before *I* fell asleep, however — the events of the evening had been too overwhelming.

The next morning, my wife felt generally well except for a feeling of tiredness, which of course is to be expected after a serious illness.

After this incident my interest in the possibility of control over body functions that we think of as "automatic" grew so intense that soon I was enrolling in every available post-graduate course in hypnotherapy. I began to fly all over the country, to wherever an interesting seminar or lecture was being given. The idea that the individual can take charge of his or her own health and healing was so exciting that I began to research the possibilities of a new form of therapy, one that the patient could practice without a therapist. Soon I was teaching my findings in various institutions and universities — wherever people were interested in learning of these potentials.

All this began fifteen years ago, but I have never ceased to be amazed at the powers of healing that lie dormant in each of us — and at the ease with which it is possible to allow the self-corrective potential to return us to the state of good health and harmony of mind and body.

Some of my more intriguing experiences with Selective Awareness Therapy have been the changes I've been able to make in my own health by practicing the techniques of Selective Awareness. I'm my own best guinea pig.

While I was growing up, I always had three or four colds a year — I caught every bug that came along. I just accepted this situation as normal and natural — as though it were "natural" to be miserable, sick, and droopy as much as two months out of every twelve! And that pattern continued into my adult life. Of course, as a doctor I couldn't take that much time off, so I used to go to work anyway, wearing a mask so my patients wouldn't catch whatever I had. But one day when I arrived at my office, sniffling and sneezing and with a sore throat, my nurse took one look at me and said, "You might as well go home and take care of yourself, because you're going to chase off all your patients anyway."

So I went home and went to bed. But then I started getting angry. Medical science might not be able to cure the common cold, but suddenly I didn't see why I had to keep on catching them like that, one right after the other. So I made myself a tape recording with a standard Selective Awareness induction. Then I shut off the tape recorder and began to explore.

I wanted to know what happened *as* I got the cold — how did I feel? Suddenly I felt a great sadness, and the words "Poor Peter" came into mind. What did that mean? "Poor Peter, you're working too hard." I quickly reviewed my schedule and saw that I was one of those doctors who thinks he can work 24 hours a day, 7 days a week, 365 days a year.

I asked myself, "What does this cold mean?"

The answer was, "I'm giving you days off, you have to take them."

"So, it's a day off I need?"

My "Yes" finger was frantically signaling, "Yes."

"Working too hard?"

"Yes."

"What if I change my schedule?"

"Yes."

"OK, if I change my schedule, do I really have to be in bed sick?"

"No."

So I made a decision to change my office hours, and then I went through a rehearsal of healing, seeing the mucosal linings of my nose and throat losing their congestion, returning to their normal healthy state. Within a short period of time my sniffles and sore throat had cleared completely, and my temperature had returned to normal. I kept the commitment I had made to myself, changed my office hours, and watched my schedule closely. That was the last cold I had for a long time — I didn't need them any more.

About three years later, though, I came down with those familiar symptoms — sore throat, sniffles, a bad cough. This time I knew it couldn't be my office hours, because I was on vacation in Europe. I decided to find out what was happening. This time, instead of sadness, I felt contempt. "Here you are in Europe, supposed to be on vacation, and you're so busy going around to lectures and clinics, you're not even leaving yourself any time to visit old friends that you haven't seen in years!" I immediately cancelled the rest of the activities I had scheduled for myself on this "vacation" trip, and had a fine time looking up and visiting several old friends with whom I had almost lost touch.

That time I really learned my lesson — and I haven't had a cold since then. When we are not in harmony with ourselves, we become vulnerable to all sorts of negative influences, including disease processes. We each have our own set of symptoms that lets us know when something's going on that we should pay attention to — mine was colds. But it's certain that when we don't listen to ourselves, nature will give us something to listen to!

Selective Awareness Therapy and Hypnosis

In my early work in research in hypnosis, I learned a great deal about the history of hypnotherapy and about the usefulness, power, and drawbacks of the classical approach to hypnotherapy.

Hypnosis has been used successfully in therapy for centuries and the popularity of the technique was at its height during the late 1800s. Sigmund Freud was a student of Jean Charcot, one of the great pioneers of hypnotherapy. Initially, Freud used hypnosis in treating hysteria and later in exploring the subconscious and unconscious mind. However, Freud did not have the talent of his master Charcot or of some of his other contemporaries. His own personal discomfort with intimate eye contact may well have been one of the reasons that Freud abandoned his work with hypnosis.

For whatever reasons, the medical profession lost interest in hypnosis during the first half of this century. The past twenty years, however, have seen a tremendous growth in the use of hypnosis in psychology, medicine, and dentistry. In 1957 the American Society for Clinical Hypnosis was formed, an organization within the American Medical Association representing over 25,000 members. The book *Psychic Discoveries Behind the Iron Curtain*, by Sheila Ostrander and Lynn Schroeder, has given the Western world a new look at the tremendous possibilities of hypnosis in many branches of science. Hypnosis has become an important tool in the treatment of conditions for which conventional medicine has no alternative or remedies.

However, hypnosis is such a powerful tool that it lends itself to misuse by the over-authoritarian therapist or the unscrupulous hypnotist, or by the clever social jester who turns it into a parlor game. The current misuse of hypnosis in movies, television, and literature has created a popular misconception about possible violation of the human rights of the patient. The prospective patient who sees a television program about the all-powerful hypnotist transforming his victim into a criminal or robot completely in the power of the hypnotist will hardly be comfortable about his hypnotherapy.

Selective Awareness Therapy has several useful and beneficial points in common with hypnotherapy. Both techniques result in a tremendous feeling of physical and mental relaxation and in the ability to enter the world of the subconscious. In fact, this ability to explore the unknown world of the mind is actually greater in Selective Awareness Therapy than in hypnotherapy. Achievement of control over "automatic" body functions is equal with both methods. The increased awareness with this method is very specific, whereas in hypnosis it is more generalized.

However, there are also many differences between hypnosis and Selective Awareness. The most important of these, of course, is that in Selective Awareness Therapy you are your own therapist. Selective Awareness Therapy differs from self-hypnosis in several important ways. For one thing, Selective Awareness Therapy purposely avoids the expectation of cure by suggestion. Instead, it gives you an increased receptivity to change, based on your own insights into the way your mind and body work together, in illness and in health.

The induction exercises in Selective Awareness Therapy avoid any connotation of sleep, unconsciousness, or trance, but allow you to let go of tension and preoccupations in a state of "super-consciousness." Because Selective Awareness Therapy encourages introspective awareness, the expectation of being passively controlled is replaced with confidence in your own ability to adjust your physical and psychological functions to normal.

Because Selective Awareness Therapy does not concern itself with "levels of depth," because you are in charge of how much of your own internal nature you wish to reveal to yourself, there is no reason to fear failure or loss of control.

Further, the state of Selective Awareness is available to anyone who is cooperative, motivated, and able to concentrate.

Another major difference between Selective Awareness Therapy and hypnosis lies in the absence of expectations that are limiting factors in hypnosis. Since your expectations, assumptions, and values are all involved in the construction of any altered state of consciousness, Selective Awareness Therapy avoids many of the negative situations of hypnosis simply by having neutral expectations. In Selective Awareness, you are always conscious, able to return instantly to the state of Social Awareness (normal awareness) for evaluation and monitoring of the self-help process.

This difference, the nonprejudiced expectation, is probably the major reason for the greater ease and comfort of Selective Awareness Therapy. As we will see, the replacement of hypnotic tests or challenges with "pretending" in Selective Awareness Therapy bypasses the critical factor of your mind (cortical evaluation and judgment), short-circuiting any anxiety about loss of control or possible failure to attain the desired state. The purpose of "bypassing the critical factor" is to stop the self-evaluative, analytical functions of the brain in order to make room for creative fantasies and healthful imagery.

Psyche and Soma — Mind and Body

We have already mentioned the concept of "mind-body harmony." An interesting question is, why should we think of them as "split," or different, in the first place? The relationship between mind and body has intrigued man for centuries. In early times, the Greek and Roman cultures attempted to deal with the phenomena of nature and of human emotions by equating them with mind and body. Psychological investigation diminished as demonology and superstition cast their spell throughout the Middle Ages. During the Renaissance, the scientific approach was championed and interest in psychological experience was viewed as a manifestation of man's more primitive past. In the seventeenth century, advances in physics and the natural sciences by such great thinkers as Newton and Galileo also awakened curiosity about the relationship between physical illness and emotional behavior patterns. In the nineteenth century, with philosophers like Descartes and Spinoza, new theories of the interaction of psyche and soma dealt largely with poetic renditions of sin and its consequences on spirit and matter.

A more systematic approach to understanding human

behavior was presented by Freud in the twentieth century. Scientific exploration of instinctual drive, especially sexual energy, gave a rational explanation for the effect of unconscious mental processes on the development of physical symptoms. Thus the evolution of the mind from instinctual arousal to emotional perception became the focus for investigations into mind-body harmony, and Freud's limited theories of instinctual drive and their relationship to the unconscious were soon challenged and modified.

While Western cultures struggled with the philosophical content of life experience and the growing body of empirical scientific data, the Chinese culture had long since begun its own investigations into psyche and soma. "Oracle bones," dating as far back as the fourteenth century B.C., were inscribed with the character names of various diseases. With the passage of thousands of years, Chinese medicine was molded by philosophical concepts with various schools of thought. Acupuncture, for example, is as valid and valuable a technique today as it was in 3000 B.C.

One area of difference between the development of Chinese and Western medicine is that, in the Oriental tradition, mind and body are not thought of as separate entities, antagonistically opposed in a struggle of domination by one with repression of the other. Chinese philosophy has always held that harmony exists when there is a balance between Yin and Yang. As night follows day, the cyclical elements of Yin and Yang create a natural flow of physical and mental energies, the disturbance of one causing a dysfunction in the other.

Whether we speak of Yin and Yang or psyche and soma, it is apparent that man has always concerned himself with concepts of the balance of mind and body in his quest for a healthy, human existence.

In the broad spectrum of experience which contributed to the evolution of twentieth-century man, the Industrial Revolution in the nineteenth century modified man's view of himself. No longer was he exclusively identified with the products of his labor. The individual became less involved with many facets of life that had previously required his personal action. The machine made life easier, reduced hard labor, and provided commodities once available only to the wealthy.

With technical advances came specialization. The concept of the master craftsman became outdated because machines could do comparable tasks in much less time. Therefore the specialist was born out of the need for specific understanding of the complexities of technical advances. In medicine, grandmother's homeopathic remedies were replaced by chemically manufactured drugs which controlled disease and its crippling effects. The medical doctor became a specialist whose presence was necessary to insure proper diagnosis and treatment of illness; most individuals could no longer comprehend either the disease or the therapy. Man became a passive recipient of the doctor's superior knowledge and experience with no possibility of self-help. Nothing in the doctor's orthodox training or the individual's experience led either to believe that one could monitor and deal with one's own health problems. Thus curative powers were relinquished entirely to the medical profession.

With growing specialization in medicine came compartmentalization and classification of disease by code number. Therapeutic procedures also were compartmentalized and given code numbers. Insurance policies, governmental agencies, and others require matching of certain disease code numbers with certain treatment code numbers and disallow any deviation from the stereotype. Mind and body are now separated, not only in different chapters, but in different code books. The perceived gap between mind and body has grown wider.

And yet there is some resistance to this trend, a swing toward a more "Oriental" way of looking at illness and health. The term "psychosomatic" was coined by Felix Deutsch in 1927. The first journal of psychosomatic medicine appeared in 1939. In 1954, the Academy of Psychosomatic Medicine was formed. This specialty of psychosomatic medicine is concerned with investigating mind-body interactions.

Some interesting experimental results in psychosomatic

medicine reveal, for example, a coincidence of the onset of diabetes with stress (Hinckel et al.). Lidz and Whitehorn found that emotional disturbance caused by troubled interpersonal relationships preceded the onset of hyperthyroidism in 90 percent of the cases in their study. Anxiety, hostility, anger, and guilt, as reactions to survival-threatening situations, were found in 65 subjects who suffered from backaches (Holmes and Wolf).

The list of such experimental results is practically endless. In short, we now know that we have the ability not only to remove the symptoms of illness from our bodies but also to induce the imbalances that cause such symptoms.

Now we can understand the dilemma of dehumanization. While the positive gains of twentieth-century medicine have brought health and longevity, we have been alienated from our own health process. Yet the powerful effect that man has on his own destiny cannot long be minimized. A more holistic approach to medicine is being created, an approach that recognizes the interaction of life situations, socio-economic factors, and emotions in the disease process. The approach also accepts that the individual is the one who must assume responsibility for his own health.

Two

Relax — Let Go — Tune In

Preparing for Selective Awareness Therapy

Now that you've read a little about what Selective Awareness is and how it works, in this chapter you will practice getting into the state of Selective Awareness, to feel what it's like and get a sense of how you can work with it.

Please remember that Selective Awareness Therapy is *not* a substitute for a thorough examination by a physician. If you are troubled by any kind of symptoms or think you may have an abnormal physical condition, see your doctor. However, there is no reason that Selective Awareness Therapy cannot be used as primary therapy or as an adjunct to any other kind of therapy, to alleviate headaches and other physical pains as well as tension and nervous stress. As you will see, you can also use Selective Awareness Therapy to quit smoking, lose weight, or improve your learning ability. Just remember that pain and other symptoms are warning signals that should never be ignored and that nothing can take the place of diagnosis and treatment by a physician.

The first step in learning to practice Selective Awareness Therapy is to choose a time of day when you won't be interrupted, when you're free to concentrate all your attention on the task of healing. You'll need at least a half hour at first, although later sessions can be conducted in ten or fifteen minutes.

Settle yourself comfortably in a chair — or, if you've practiced meditation, in any position you've found to be good for sitting still and concentrating. It's better not to lie down — you don't want to get *too* relaxed and fall asleep.

Make sure you're not wearing any tight clothing. Tight clothing can actually restrict or block the flow of energy in your body. Pay particular attention to your hands. When you're in a state of Selective Awareness your fingers and wrists should be lying loose and relaxed, free to move in any direction.

Now that you're relaxed and comfortable, read over the first Selective Awareness exercise. You may want to read the exercise out loud two or three times until you are completely familiar with it.

After you've read the exercise, you may want to make a tape recording of it. (Or you may ask a friend to make the recording for you — some people find that they are bothered by the sound of their own voice.) As you read through the exercise again, picture yourself making a tape recording of it. Note the timing you will use, your tone of voice, and where you will want to leave pauses. The recording will be about 10 to 15 minutes long. You can leave pauses in the recording where you think you'll need time to follow the instructions. You will soon find that you can adjust the recorder without disturbing your state of Selective Awareness. In fact, the act of switching the tape recorder on and off can actually be used to deepen your awareness.

Bypassing Your Judgment Factor

Remember that in Selective Awareness Therapy it is important to bypass cortical scrutiny. This means getting past that part of the brain that's always judging things, or figuring them out, telling you yes and no, should and shouldn't.

One method for getting past the critical factor is to play the game of pretend, as you will do in the first Selective Awareness exercise. You may pretend, for instance, that you can't open your eyes, effectively telling your cortex, "Just relax for a moment, I know that this is actually a fantasy." You will learn to participate fully in the game of pretend, and to develop healthful fantasies about yourself. You must bypass that critical factor — the "reality factor" — to make room for the fantasies that you can develop for evaluation and treatment. In bypassing cortical activity, you are giving yourself a chance to work in Selective Awareness without continually judging, criticizing, and evaluating what's going on. So if you find yourself continually asking, "How am I doing?" or "What's this all about?" relax and redirect that energy into concentration.

After you have finished the exercise and returned to Social Awareness (regular consciousness), write down what you have experienced — how you felt, what you were aware of, whether it seems relevant or not. This doesn't need to be extensive — just jot down a few notes that are meaningful to you about the experience of Selective Awareness. Or you may want to write pages and pages — it's up to you.

Each time you do an exercise you will be bombarded with new insights that may or may not appear to be relevant to the problem or area of your body that you're working with. These flashes of insight won't be limited to the times just after you practice. When something new occurs to you, take a moment to write it down, whatever you're doing, whether you're at your office or at the kitchen sink.

Very soon, this Personal History notebook will be a remarkable document of personal growth and adventure of Selective Awareness Therapy.

As you make progress in Selective Awareness, your friends and relatives will notice and comment on how well you're looking. If they're interested in learning more about what you've been doing to cause such dramatic change, show them this book and tell them all about it — but don't play your tapes for them. Selective Awareness is a personal kind of therapy, and what works for you might only be confusing for someone else.

To review — here are the steps to follow in your first

Selective Awareness exercise:
1. Get comfortable.
2. Read the induction.
3. Study and learn the material you need for the induction and/or make your tape.
4. Sit back comfortably and let your mind go over the exercise, or listen to the tape. (You may want to do this in another session, or the next day. The timing is up to you.)
5. What was your experience of Selective Awareness like? What did you feel? How do you feel now? Write it down.

Let Go — Enjoy Selective Awareness

(If you're using a tape recorder, do not record the parts of the Induction that are in parentheses.)

Look up toward your eyebrows and keep on looking up while you allow your eyelids to close. (You'll feel some stress on your eyes and if you are doing it properly the lids will probably flutter a little as you are closing them.)

Take a deep breath now, as you close your eyes. With your eyes closed, focus your attention on something pleasant, something that is not related to any problems that may be on your mind. (You may think of lying on a sunny beach, or walking through a green meadow, or skiing down a mountain. Allow all your senses to play with the scene you are creating for yourself. Smell the flowers in the meadow, feel the breeze in your face. You may want to put the scene in the tape, or just leave a pause for your mind to construct the scene. Whatever you are doing, do it so clearly and vividly that you can see it in color and motion.) When you are fully there in the scene, take another deep breath, and as you let it out give yourself the signal, "Now relax." Stay with the picture you have created; give all your concentration and attention to that image.

To help your body relax, begin to let go with all of the muscles on top of your head. Feel the muscles go limp and loose in your forehead. Now allow your eyes, eyebrows, and eyelids to relax. If your eyelids begin to flutter a little, that's all right. Just let them relax.

Send that feeling of relaxation into the rest of your face, your cheeks and jaws. Let go of all the tension you are holding in your jaw. Let your jaw relax until your teeth just barely touch. Now allow your neck and shoulders to relax. As the tension drains from your body you get further and further inside yourself, becoming more and more aware of your body. Drift deeper and deeper, allowing that feeling of relaxation to spread all the way down your arms to your fingers.

Imagine that you can follow the air inside your lungs and let go of all the tightness that is held there. Feel the muscles around your stomach become relaxed. Allow that deepening relaxation to spread into your pelvis, your hips and your thighs, drifting deeper and deeper, deeper inside yourself, acquiring more and more inner peace. Drifting, drifting, deeper and deeper.

Now let that feeling of relaxation spread to your thighs, to your calves, and to the soles of your feet and to your toes, until you have the feeling that your whole body is wrapped in a blanket of relaxation. Deeper and deeper, drifting deeper and deeper, allowing all parts of your body to completely and totally relax. Remember that deeper means getting more in touch with yourself, more in tune with your body, more aware of your feelings and your body and yourself.

Now as you count slowly from ten to zero, any lingering tension in your body will be discharged, to be replaced by deep peace and comfort.

Ten — let yourself relax now, deeper and deeper.

Nine — any last bit of tension in your body can now be allowed to evaporate.

Eight — drifting way down, deeper and deeper.

Seven — comfortable, relaxed.

Six, five, four, three — way down deep.

Two, one, and zero.

Now take a moment to enjoy the sensation of deep peace and healthful relaxation that has spread throughout your body.

Pretend that your eyelids are heavy, so heavy that they just simply won't function. On the count of one, pretend that your eyes will not open; two, imagine your eyelids are stuck together tight; three, test whether or not you can open your eyes, to make sure your fantasies are winning.

Every time a thought comes into your mind you don't want to be there, don't fight it. Simply pretend that you can't open your eyes, and let the thought leave your mind, allowing you to become even more relaxed, going deeper and deeper all the time.

Notice how relaxed and comfortable you feel. And the next time you do the exercise, you will be able to go very quickly into this very comfortable, deep state of relaxation.

When you count to five, let yourself come up feeling comfortable, good, full of positive energy.

One — let yourself come up.

Two — feeling really good and relaxed.

Three — you know that the next time you practice Selective Awareness you will be able to relax even more easily. Now begin to open your eyes.

Four — feeling very alert, and

Five — refreshed, relaxed, comfortable, feeling good all over.

When you return to the state of Social Awareness, note how good you feel, how relaxed and alert you are. Other people may notice, too, and comment on how well you look, because the absence of tension in the facial muscles makes a dramatic difference in appearance.

Be sure to write down all the impressions you received during your first venture into Selective Awareness. You may have questions the first couple of times you do the practice. That's fine — write them down. All of your impressions are material to work with in future Selective Awareness exercises, and simply recognizing your own emotional state can be therapeutic.

Try to find time to do the first Selective Awareness exercise twice a day until you're able to slip easily and quickly into the state of Selective Awareness. You may be able to do this immediately, in a couple of days, or it may take a week. Remember that this ability is the foundation of Selective Awareness Therapy, and give yourself the compassion to keep at it. It won't be too hard, because just giving yourself the time and attention to slow down and relax twice a day will in itself have very beneficial effects. And eventually you will be able to enter Selective Awareness whenever you wish, without using a lengthy induction.

Increasing Your Selective Awareness Skills

When you feel that you're completely comfortable with the state of Selective Awareness, go on to the following exercise, which will introduce two important elements of Selective Awareness Therapy — *ideomotor finger signals* and *image rehearsal.*

Ideomotor Finger Signals

Ideomotor finger signals allow you to communicate with your inner self while you're in a state of Selective Awareness. The best way to understand these signals is to practice them. But knowing a little about how they work is also helpful.

These signals will give you information about internal states and internal memories that ordinarily do not reach consciousness. This internal language will also give you information about changes that are occurring within you during the following Selective Awareness practices using image rehearsal.

Ideomotor finger signals may be viewed as genuine communications from your inner mind, the subconscious, or the unknown. They are subtle, spontaneous, and give information about inner values, assumptions, and expectations that may be in conflict with conscious understanding. They allow you to bypass the rationalizations that often interfere with your ability to get in touch with your feelings.

These finger signals are a means of listening, of communication with your inner self. As you become fluent in this internal language, you are better able to deal with the hidden assumptions that ordinarily escape your conscious scrutiny.

Image Rehearsal

Image rehearsal is a technique of Selective Awareness Therapy that offers an immediate alteration of both psychological and physiological symptoms. You can use image rehearsal in Selective Awareness Therapy for training, de-conditioning, and for becoming familiar with creative alternatives in your life. Once you are able to rehearse the way you would like to be, you will be able to gain control over many of your problems.

Through image rehearsal you will learn to see yourself not only in the past but in present and future events as well. When you establish a positive self-image in Selective Awareness, that image continues to work all the time to effect change in the direction you choose. Instead of a constant negative thought-mind battle, you'll have a positive self-image that continues to work automatically because you've trained it in the state of Selective Awareness.

This is what you are really after, a change of attitude as well as a change of physical behavior, because *therapy means change.* Image rehearsal is a powerful tool in effecting that change. Let's suppose that the symptom you're working on is headaches, and that through Selective Awareness you have understood that your pain is connected with fear. Using the ideomotor finger signals, you've also asked for and received permission to get rid of the fear and pain because these symptoms are no longer necessary. Using image rehearsal, you then see yourself going through the symptom-producing events that have caused the fear and headaches in the first place. And you see yourself painlessly handling situations that ordinarily would bring on a headache. In this way image rehearsal of a desired result allows you to desensitize and de-condition yourself.

You will also learn to practice image rehearsal in the future, seeing yourself perhaps a year from now, still free of headaches and other symptoms. This positive future image rehearsal helps to increase your belief that you can indeed achieve harmony of mind and body.

The actual practice of image rehearsal will be introduced gradually, starting with the next exercise. So now go ahead and read the second Selective Awareness induction, noting the introduction of the two new elements of ideomotor finger signals and image rehearsal. You will also notice that the basic induction, getting into the state of Selective Awareness, is different from the one you've been using. This is to demonstrate that the actual words aren't important, but are only a focus for allowing your mind to slip into Selective Awareness.

After you've read the second induction exercise a couple of times and/or made your tape, get comfortable, and again remember to pay special attention to allowing your wrists and fingers to relax as you do the exercise.

Tuning In — Practice

Take a deep breath and as you let it out close your eyes. Close them with the single purpose of letting yourself be so completely and totally relaxed that nothing is more important than this complete mind and body relaxation.

Let go of your mind, let it go wherever it wants to go. Let it go floating along as you take another breath and as you let it out just let your body go along. Let all your muscles relax and go limp and loose by simply giving yourself the signal, "Now relax."

Now let go of all the tension in your muscles. Notice how good it feels when your forehead relaxes and your skull relaxes. Notice how good it feels when your eyes feel restful and relaxed, with just a gentle flutter from time to time. And as you breathe let your cheeks and your jaw relax. Let that feeling of relaxation extend inside and down your throat. As that feeling of muscular release flows down your throat let your neck relax. Let your neck relax, the sides and the front and the back of your neck. Just allow that feeling of letting go to move into your shoulders and down your arms, your upper arms, your forearms and all the way down to your fingers and to every muscle from your head down into your shoulders and your arms. Just completely and totally relax.

Now tune in to the rhythm of your breathing. Let your breathing work for you, soothing and relaxing any remaining areas of tension. Let it automatically relax all the muscles in your chest. As you take a deep breath and let it out, let that feeling of relaxation also extend into your stomach, relaxing and letting go. Take another deep breath and push it all the way to your pelvis until your pelvis relaxes, your buttocks relax, all the muscles in your thighs, your calves, the soles of your feet and your toes, until you feel that relaxation reaching right down to the tips of your toes.

Let the rhythm of your breathing take you deeper and deeper inside yourself, into a deeper and deeper awareness of your own body.

Every time a thought occurs that you don't want there, don't fight it. Let it come in and let it go out. Simply pretend that you can't open your eyes, and let your fantasy take over, allowing you always to go deeper and deeper in awareness.

Now pretend that you can't open your eyes, and imagine that you see the word "Yes" on a big signboard directly in front of you. When you can see that big "Yes" quite clearly, you'll find that one of your fingers will begin to move. Think the word "Yes" so clearly to yourself that before you know it, one of your fingers begins to move. Affirmation. Consent. YES. Yes. Yes. Just think the word to yourself and allow your arms to be free, your hands to be free, your fingers to be free, and something will happen. "Yes." Pay no attention to anything else, just think "Yes." Yes to letting go, yes to total relaxation. Now feel quite clearly the connection between that finger movement and the feeling of affirmation — "Yes!"

Envision the signboard again, but now the word "No!" is written on it. "No, no, no, no, no, no!" See what your fingers are saying. One finger will move — a different finger this time. Now you've found your "No" finger. Feel quite clearly the connection between that finger movement and the feeling of denial — "No!"

Now go back to your "Yes" finger. Let it signal consent. Practice the feeling of "Yes," and listen to what your finger is telling you about your deep feeling of contentment and relaxation. Every time your "Yes" finger signals affirmation, allow yourself to go a little deeper into awareness of yourself. See yourself feeling good, relaxed and alert, full of energy and enjoying just being alive. When you see yourself quite clearly, feeling comfortable and alert and relaxed, allow your "Yes" finger to signal again.

"Yes" — consent. Yes to feeling good about yourself. When you "Yes" finger tells you that you're ready, begin to come up to a state of Social Awareness. Begin to count to five, and let yourself come up feeling just like that, just as your imagination is producing the feeling for you now. See yourself feeling comfortable, good, full of positive energy.

One — let yourself come up.

Two — feeling really good and relaxed.

Three — you know that the next time you practice Selective Awareness you will be able to relax more easily than ever before.

Four — begin to open your eyes.

Five — refreshed, relaxed, comfortable, feeling good all over — just as you had envisioned.

Now that you've returned to the state of Social Awareness, write down how you felt during the experience, and how you're feeling now. Did you enjoy using a different induction to get into Selective Awareness? Did your fingers respond to the idea of consent and denial? Remember to write in your Personal History notebook every time you practice.

If your "Yes" and "No" fingers didn't respond this first time, don't worry about it. The ideomotor finger signals make such a deep connection with the subconscious mind that it may take a little time to establish them. Just continue to do the exercise twice a day, and concentrate on relaxing your wrists and fingers. Sometimes the signal may be a tiny muscular twitch, or you may find your fingers waving wildly. Everybody is different.

But what if you've practiced the second exercise several times, feel sure that you're comfortably in Selective Awareness, but still haven't got in touch with your "Yes" and "No" fingers? In that case, simply choose a finger to be your "Yes" finger, and move it consciously at the appropriate times in the exercise. Do the same for your "No" finger — choose it and move it consciously. This will allow the connection to be made at a deep level, and after two or three practice sessions you will find that your fingers will be moving spontaneously. You may also find it helpful to open your eyes and watch your fingers moving.

After you're thoroughly familiar with the use of the ideomotor finger signals, you will find that every time your "Yes" finger signals, it actually "calls up" more information, and allows your mind to make room for that information.

Preparing for Image Rehearsal

Once the ideomotor finger signals are firmly established as a means of communication with yourself, it's time to learn a third exercise, one with several purposes:

1. to introduce a third induction, one that allows you to get in touch with your breathing to deepen your state of Selective Awareness;

2. to strengthen your response to the ideomotor finger signals and image rehearsal; and

3. to introduce another Selective Awareness technique — consider, consult, consent.

Consider, consult, consent is a checking device that you use on yourself every step of the way — to monitor your progress and to make sure that your mind and body are cooperating fully for health and harmony. The system works like this. While you are in the state of Selective Awareness, consider how you would like to change. Then consult with yourself — is it all right to change? Listen to what your mind and body are telling you, to what the finger signals are saying. And finally, consent to the change, through image rehearsal and other Selective Awareness techniques.

Of course, you may not consent to every change that you consider. If you consult and receive a negative response, "No, it's not all right to change," then other Selective Awareness techniques may be applied to get at the symptom-producing events and clear away the energy blocks that are preventing change. We'll consider some of these techniques later.

For now, read through the following Selective Awareness exercise, study it and/or make your tape, and get comfortable to do the practice.

Using Image Rehearsal

(If you are using a tape recorder, do not record the parts of the exercise that are in parentheses.)

Take a deep breath and as you let it out allow yourself to go to a place that is totally relaxing, where your mind is completely relaxed. Go to a place where the atmosphere is not only relaxing but also healing and focus all your senses on that positive, pleasant image. You have no need to respond to external stimuli now, so turn all your attention inward, inside yourself. Take another deep breath and follow it all the way into your lungs. As you let it out give your body the signal, "Now relax." Say mentally to yourself — "Now relax." As you hear yourself saying, "Now relax," you will find that your "Yes" finger will move. Allow yourself to take that "Yes" finger movement as a way of letting out negative preoccupations from your mind.

Now begin to let go with all your muscles. Begin with your feet. Let your feet become comfortable and light as all the muscles go loose and relaxed, drifting, drifting. Every time a muscle lets go into relaxation, allow your "Yes" finger to move.

And each movement of your "Yes" finger will help you to go deeper and deeper into your own body, so that as your legs relax, and your thighs relax, you begin to experience a very comfortable sensation of floating and drifting.

Take another deep breath and imagine that this breath is drawn downward and relaxes the area of your genitals and your buttocks and your pelvis, and all your organs inside. Let that feeling of relaxation rise upward, rising, soaring, drifting, sweeping you up and along into a very comfortable and relaxed place.

As you take another deep breath and let it out, notice how good it feels as your chest relaxes and you become aware of all the organs inside your body letting go, letting go and drifting deeper.

Take another deep breath and as you let it out become aware of a kind of symphony of relaxation in your chest and stomach and pelvis, feeling all your inner organs relax as well. And let the feeling of relaxation rise upward into your throat. Feel it swelling upward, surging upward, spreading into your shoulders. As it spreads across your shoulders feel it rise into your jaw, your tongue, your cheeks. Let your jaw feel comfortable and relaxed, and relax the area around your eyes and face, until you have the feeling that relaxation has reached the top of your head. A very comfortable sensation is pulling your body upward so that now your arms, your forearms, and fingers are comfortable and relaxed.

As you count backward from ten to zero, let your "Yes" finger signal each deeper stage of relaxation. Let each number be a symbol of rising relaxation as you go deeper inside yourself, becoming more relaxed and more comfortable.

Ten — drifting deeper and deeper.

Nine — at the same time rising higher and higher.

Eight, seven, six — drifting deeper and deeper.

Five, four — notice how your "Yes" finger is signaling a deeper state of relaxation.

Three, two, one, and zero.

Allow yourself to pretend that you can't open your eyes.

And remember that each time your "Yes" finger signals, the state of Selective Awareness will be intensified.

Now consider how you would like to feel when you return to Social Awareness. (Pick a particular state or quality you would like to experience, such as "relaxed," or "alert," or a general feeling of well-being. Don't try to concentrate on solving any particular problem yet, but just choose a state to practice in Selective Awareness. You can substitute whatever you choose for the words "well-being," "comfortable," "relaxed," etc.) Feel yourself now, comfortable and relaxed, a state of well-being spreading throughout your body and mind. Picture yourself as you would like to feel in a few minutes, when you return to Social Awareness.

Consult with yourself. Would it be all right to feel good, to feel relaxed and comfortable in body and mind? Allow your "Yes" finger to signal consent. Yes, it's OK to enjoy that wonderful feeling of well-being. Allow your "Yes" finger to signal that you are getting a really clear visual and emotional image of yourself as you choose to be.

Now, as you begin to return to the state of Social Awareness, hold in your mind the image of yourself, the feelings of well-being and comfort that you are experiencing.

Begin now to count from one to five.

One — let yourself begin to come up.

Two — feeling good, relaxed.

Three — whenever you're ready, open your eyes.

Four — wide awake now.

Five — feeling alert, refreshed, and relaxed, just as you have been imagining.

Now once again write down your experience of Selective Awareness, including any stray thoughts that cross your mind.

As with the ideomotor finger signals, don't worry if you get no response, or a negative response, to the question, "Would it be all right to feel good?" Just keep practicing until your fingers signal consent. Because of course you *do* want to feel good and to allow your mind and body to work together in harmony.

How Image Rehearsal Can Change Your Life

Sometimes just one session of image rehearsal in Selective Awareness is enough to get in touch with and eliminate long-standing problems. Ron came to me because his inability to speak to groups of more than two or three people was hampering his career. In the state of Selective Awareness, he oriented back to only one symptom-producing event — a childhood experience he had almost forgotten, but which had affected his entire style of relating to more than one person at a time.

It seems that every year, from the age of eight to twelve, Ron had been forced to play "Jingle Bells" on the trumpet at the church Christmas social. Convinced that everyone in the audience was laughing at him, he felt humiliated. As an adult, he was unable to perform in front of groups in any capacity at all.

When he made the connection between his childhood humiliation and his present inability, Ron became very angry and stated, "I'm going to break that damn trumpet!" Although the original trumpet was long gone, he did smash it in image rehearsal, over and over again, until his anger over his forced performance was released. He then went back over each of those traumatic Christmas socials, seeing himself standing on the stage playing "Jingle Bells" for his own enjoyment and to the delight of his audience.

Finally, Ron rehearsed an image of himself in the future, delivering a report to a large group of people at work, a group that included his boss and the president of the company. He saw himself speaking fluently and clearly, enjoying his own confidence in his knowledge of the subject.

That one session was all that Ron needed to overcome his fear of public speaking. He continued to practice image rehearsal for other problem areas in his life, and a few months later, he received the promotion for which he had been waiting three years.

Giving Yourself Positive Feedback

Any time you practice image rehearsal in Selective Awareness, you can expect positive change very soon. In Ron's case, for example, an inability to address groups of people cleared up after only one session. As soon as you notice change in the area you're working on, give yourself positive feedback. Concentrate on every detail of your progress and on your mastery of the techniques of Selective Awareness. After all, being your own therapist is something to be proud of! And remember that the more positive feedback you give yourself, the quicker and more effective the process of self-healing will be.

The following excerpts are from a positive feedback tape made by a patient who had succeeded in reducing his blood pressure to a safe level after having required medication for over ten years. As you will notice, his style of "talking to himself" is different from what you will find in the exercises in this book. But then yours probably is, too. Remember that the printed exercises are only guidelines and that, as you become proficient in Selective Awareness Therapy, your imagination is the only limit to what you can do with these techniques.

Excerpts from a Positive Feedback Tape

"Now, Jack, for a moment I would like for you just to tune in to what the doctor said after he had a look at your arteries. How good they look! I want you to become really aware that this is the product of the work you have been doing with yourself. Just look at those arteries! I'm really proud of you. Just remember that your blood pressure is low now, and it can stay low. No need to get excited and let that blood pressure shoot up anymore.

"Now just say thank you for that ability to internalize the concepts of medicine, which at the time you began was all new and yet it made a lot of sense, and still does. And thank those arteries and kidneys, too, for doing such a great job."

You get the idea. When you're pleased with yourself, with the work you've done, or with a part of your body, let yourself know how grateful you are.

Three

The Nervous Systems and Emotions

To make the best use of the techniques offered by Selective Awareness Therapy, you'll need to understand something about how your body works and about the interactions between your emotions and physical functioning. What you don't know *can* hurt you, or at least make it more difficult for you to help your mind and body return to a natural state of harmony. Understanding the automatic functioning of the body leads to greater control over one's state of health.

In this chapter we will take a look at the autonomic nervous system and the central nervous system, to see how bodily functions are normally controlled and how they can break down, causing physical illness. We will also examine the relationship between emotions and health.

The Autonomic Nervous System (ANS)

The autonomic nervous system is part of the inner structure of the brain. The communication system of the ANS consists of two long groups of nerve cells, running down either side of the spine, with connecting nerve fibers to the brain and to the different organs of the body. The two parts of the ANS, the sympathetic and parasympathetic nervous systems, normally act in a state of balanced opposition to each other.

The ANS is very important in regulating the functions of the body, for no organ or gland can work without the appropriate

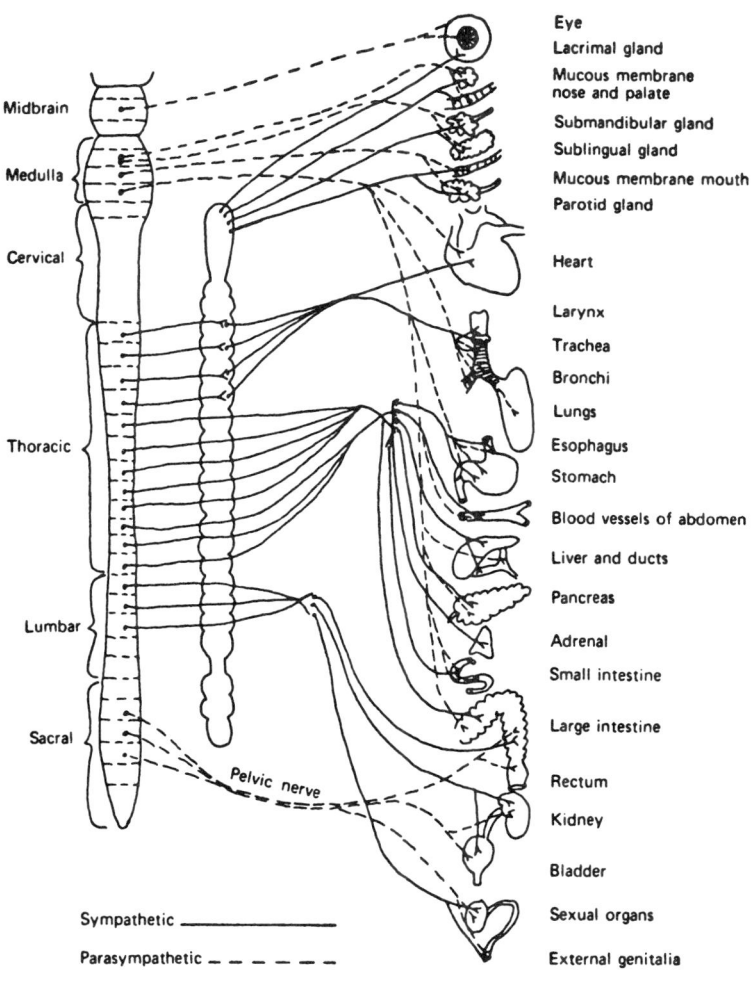

Midbrain

Medulla

Cervical

Thoracic

Lumbar

Sacral

Pelvic nerve

Eye
Lacrimal gland
Mucous membrane
nose and palate
Submandibular gland
Sublingual gland
Mucous membrane mouth
Parotid gland

Heart

Larynx

Trachea

Bronchi

Lungs

Esophagus
Stomach

Blood vessels of abdomen

Liver and ducts

Pancreas

Adrenal
Small intestine

Large intestine

Rectum

Kidney

Bladder

Sexual organs

External genitalia

Sympathetic _____

Parasympathetic _ _ _ _ _ _

Autonomic Nervous System

47

orders from this system. The ANS controls all those muscles, organs, and glands that are independent of will and not under voluntary control. Under normal conditions, the activities of the tear and sweat glands, the digestive system, the pupil of the eye, the heart and blood vessels, and the respiratory system, as well as the gastrointestinal and genitourinary tracts, are carried out quite automatically without the need of any conscious direction at all.

How Emotions Influence Your Body

The emotional state of fear produces an "adrenergic" reaction, as though the body had received a shot of adrenaline. Fear stimulates the sympathetic nervous system, which is primarily concerned with preparing the body to deal with the conditions of stress, such as in "flight or fight." At such times the heart rate is greatly increased, pumping more blood into the muscles. The blood pressure rises because the blood vessels near the surface of the body are constricted and there is greater resistance to the circulation. The blood vessels in the heart, unlike those of the rest of the body, are actually dilated. Glycogen stored in the liver is changed into glucose, which is used in muscular work. The lungs take in more air than usual, providing extra oxygen. The pupils are dilated to let in extra light and enable the person to see the danger more clearly. The sympathetic nervous system also inhibits movement of the bowel by closing the sphincters and stopping digestion of food. Similarly, contraction of the bladder sphincter closes the bladder. Finally, under conditions of fear or worry, the blood supply to the sexual organs is diminished and sexual desire is lost.

On the other side of this balanced autonomic nervous system, the emotional state of anger produces a biochemical reaction which partially stimulates the parasympathetic nervous system. The parasympathetic nervous system is generally antagonistic to the sympathetic and produces opposite actions. Stimulation of this system constricts the pupils, slows the heart and respiration, and inhibits the sphincters of the intestines and bladders while stimulating the digestion and absorption of food. Normally, the sex organs are well supplied with blood under the influence of this system and therefore easily stimulated.

The emotional state of anger mimics in part these responses in the body. However, once the biochemical response to the emotional state has been triggered, it is not under voluntary control — you may be able to control the outward manifestations of your fear or anger, but the inner biochemical response is still doing its work. Unless catharsis occurs — unless the emotions find release — the resulting chemical imbalance may cause physical illness.

Normally, the two systems of the ANS respond in reciprocal harmony to maintain a positive mind-body balance and to handle the requirements of any situation. When the complexity of the delicately balanced system is considered, however, it is easy to understand how anything that upsets this balance can lead to a large number of widely varied disorders.

Evolution of the Central Nervous System (CNS)

The central nervous system, or CNS, composed of the cortex, or outer layer of the brain, and the spinal cord, is primarily concerned with conscious evaluation, memory, emotion, and voluntary motor activity. Beneath the cortex lies the subcortex, which controls all the autonomic functions of life. The ANS is part of the subcortical apparatus. The interaction of the ANS and CNS can best be understood by looking at how they evolved.

The basic instinct of early man was survival. This instinct acted directly on the ANS by way of sympathetic and parasympathetic communication. The cortex (the outer layer of the brain, part of the central nervous system) was not sufficiently developed to interfere with the life-saving functions of "fight or flight." This ANS response was healthy and important. With further development of the human brain came the development

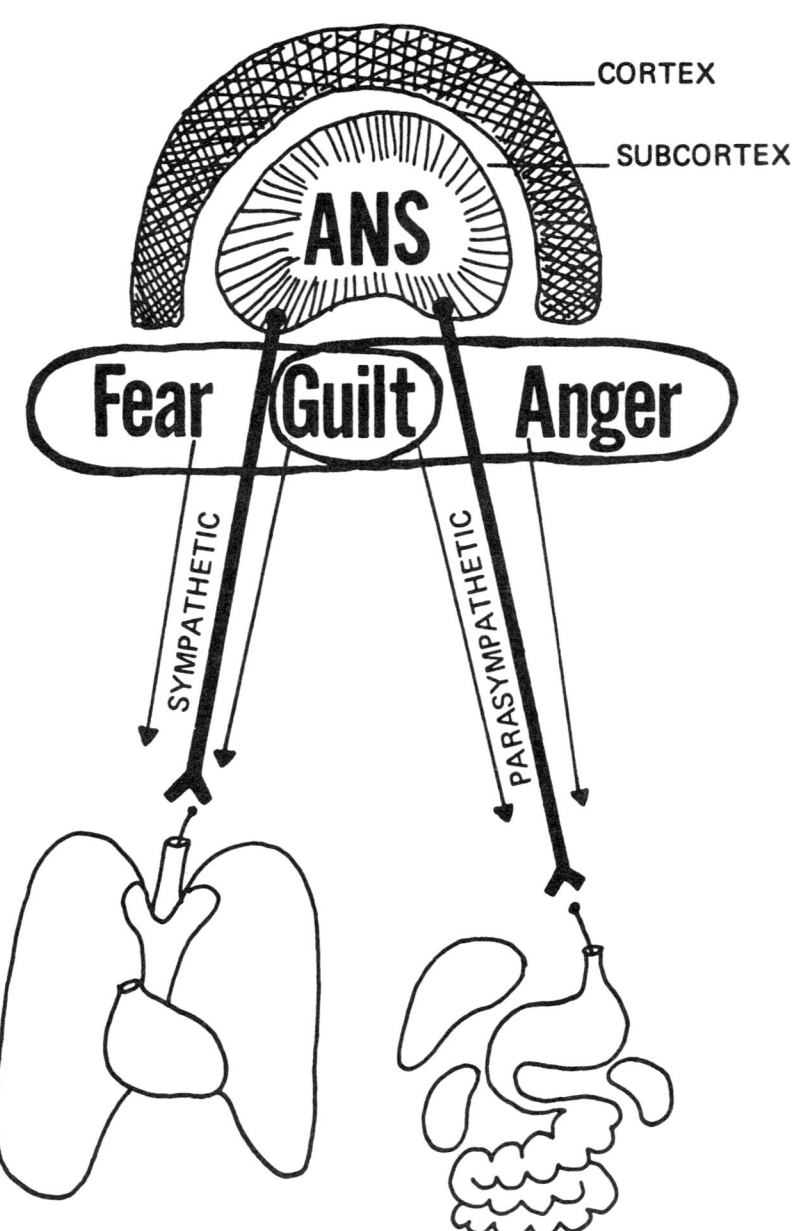

Diagram showing the influences of emotions upon the sympathetic and parasympathetic branches of the autonomic nervous system.

of the mind and the addition of emotion to instinct. With the development of civilization and urbanization man came under a third influence, the rules and regulations of groups of people living together — society. No longer was it appropriate to show emotions without regard to their consequences. Cultural and religious values added another emotion, one that is strictly man-made and not seen in animals — guilt. The once-instinctive regulation of the body by the ANS became more sophisticated; individual and cultural values and assumptions broadened the range of emotional responses while denying them an immediate outlet.

The Evolution of Emotions

Emotions, as we have seen, are the product of cortical modification of primitive instincts.

For reasons of simplicity, I'll discuss only three emotions here. These three, however, are the "heavyweights" that interfere with mind-body interaction: fear, anger, and guilt — in all their various forms. Some variations of these three basic emotions are:

Concern	Sullenness	Embarrassment
Worry	Resentment	Shame
Fretting	Frustration	Regret
FEAR	**ANGER**	**GUILT**
Panic	Rage	

Fear

With the development of the brain, fear evolved from a basic survival instinct. The emotion of fear releases a chemical substance called norepinephrine, or adrenaline, which acts upon the sympathetic fibers of the ANS and on the various internal organs. This chemical, acting on the sympathetic nervous system, aids the body in preparation for flight. When action results, for example when the individual runs away, catharsis — the release of the emotion — occurs, and the chemical is used up.

When modern man experiences fear, however, the cortex of the brain and the CNS modify the emotional response, and the intellectual evaluative process intervenes to dictate the course of action. When the cortex censors fear messages on a subconscious level, fear may never mature into a proper response that reaches catharsis, or discharge. This effect may be experienced as subtle anxiety, nervousness, or insomnia, or it may include physical symptoms, such as muscle spasm or stomach ache. But when the cortex recognizes fear or its physical result, catharsis may occur because of insight into the *thought-emotion-physical symptom complex.*

Anger

Like fear, anger has evolved out of man's survival instinct and has also been modified according to social expectation. Anger stimulates the ANS, involving both the sympathetic and parasympathetic systems, supporting the instinct for fight rather than flight.

Most people fear showing anger or experiencing the anger of others. This reluctance was important to primitive man, for whom meeting the consequences of anger was physically dangerous.

In our culture, the results of anger can be equally disastrous, although not usually directly on the physical level. If anger is stored rather than released, the resulting sullen behavior can create an emotional block between individuals. Stored anger becomes a distancing emotion, leading to harbored resentment against the "enemy" — who may be wife, husband, or any other person or group of people. Then, as in the case of fear, there is no healthy discharge of the emotion, and again physical illness may result.

Guilt

Guilt does not have the evolutionary origin of fear and anger and does not arise out of primitive survival instinct. Instead, it is the result of man's evaluations and judgments based on social customs, expectations, and values. Guilt is man-made and is the product of a violation of values, leading to shame and pain. Because our culture is based so much on reward and punishment, guilt requires for its release the understanding of and compassion for self as well as a revision of assumptions and values. Guilt is frequently accompanied by fear — fear of the consequences of the violation — and also by anger. Anger accompanied by guilt may be turned inward as self-blame, or outward at some other person or external force: "I'm no good," or, "It's all your fault, you made me do it."

The biochemical response to the emotional state of guilt may be complex, and the resulting imbalance, if no emotional outlet is found, can be destructive.

As we have seen, man's primitive instincts sent sensory messages to his undeveloped cortex, and these stimuli sent the proper responses to his ANS for "flight or fight." As the cortex developed, such instincts were modified by more refined, sophisticated emotional responses to stimuli on two levels: conscious and unconscious. These two levels functioned harmoniously, allowing the unconscious value system to modify incoming stimuli according to its desired conscious emotional response. Thus, man became a complex being, not always aware of the unconscious direction of his emotional response.

Emotional Imbalance

The following three examples show how emotions trigger automatic functions of the body. In each case, an employee asks for a raise, which is denied. The examples have been simplified to show the response of the body to either fear or anger, but in most cases what is experienced is a combination of both. How well the individual recognizes his unconscious and emotional response to the situation is the key to balance or imbalance.

Fear Imbalance — Stress

An employee needs and deserves a raise, but is indecisive about asking for it. Although intellectually he is convinced of his competence, he becomes increasingly anxious about confronting his employer. This anxiety produces a response in the autonomic nervous system releasing chemicals that cause him to tremble and perspire. Unconscious emotions of poor self-esteem cause further anxiety. On a conscious level these emotions surface as memories of past crises in which the employee was told he "would never amount to anything." Without evaluating the content of this emotional process, he is unable to acknowledge his self-worth. His composure is fractured.

The dialogue with the employer seems inconsequential. Overly polite and apologetic, the employee never actually states his reasons for wanting a raise. Instead, he minimizes them, pointing out areas in which he lacks achievement. Although the employer is reassuring, the employee is sure that the boss will now take his incompetence into consideration in granting a salary increase. Thus the tone of the interview is negative and further confirms the employee's attitude toward himself as a "cowering idiot."

The emotional outcome is frustration. Instead of a dialogue concerning the employee's factual strengths, it has become the feared confrontation of past experience. Embarrassment about the negative presentation, shame for his inability to speak up, guilt for incompetence on the job — all increase the employee's emotional anxiety. The employee achieves no catharsis or emotional release and his body keeps producing adrenaline in anticipation of a further crisis. His pulse maintains its rapid pace, causing dizziness and lightheadedness, and his intestines become vulnerable to such nervous disorders as colitis and spasm.

Unresolved emotional anxiety sets up an unconscious system of self-abuse, negatively affecting his physical functioning. Emotional turmoil becomes the overriding factor in his state of health.

Emotions act as message-carriers in the cortex, which produces the proper response in the ANS. The resulting physical symptom is a healthy signal. It is the individual's gauge in measuring unresolved emotions that need to be evaluated for mental and physical health. Ill health occurs when the emotional content of physical symptoms is ignored. This is why it is crucial to understand the mind-body interaction if the proper biological balance is to be maintained.

Anger Imbalance — Stress

As in the previous case, an employee anticipates asking for a raise, which he knows he deserves. But in this case, fear of rejection causes anger. His unconscious value system interferes with his conscious thought process. Remembering a past experience when he was unjustly fired, he becomes antagonistic toward his present employer. He becomes more and more angry, until finally he is in a rage. This message of rage is sent to the ANS, which instinctively responds with the command, "Fight." The dialogue between employer and employee takes place on an emotionally charged level. Hostility escalates to the point where neither employee nor employer understands the intensity of the anger. The employee is no longer responding to the present situation but to the more complex unconscious motivations of anger and past experience. Consequently, the employer tells him that he may get a raise if money becomes available, but cautions the employee to control his temper.

The emotional outcome of this situation is frustration. "If only I had remained calm," is the conscious thought. Embarrassment for a poor presentation, shame for the temper tantrum, guilt over false accusations — all increase the employee's anger at himself and his employer, and no catharsis takes place.

The emotional valve does not shut down, and so neither does the biochemical response of the ANS. As a result, stomach acid increases, producing ulcers and gastritis. The body is now functioning in accordance with the unresolved emotion of anger.

Healthy Stress

The third employee also wants a raise, which he knows he deserves. In this case, the instincts of fear and anger become the more complex emotions of anxiety and challenge. Anxiety triggers a chemical response in the body, stimulating the blood supply to the brain and tapping the employee's energy reserves. The corresponding emotional challenge prepares him to "stand his ground" and to focus on the immediate situation. A more harmonious balance of these automatic bodily responses allows the employee to present himself well. He knows he deserves the raise because he has intellectually reviewed his concept of self-worth in the job situation. He has also become aware of and evaluated his unconscious value system, which includes anxiety and fear of rejection, as well as resentment of authority.

This dialogue between employee and employer takes place on a rational level. The employer denies the request, but assures the employee that when profits rise he will grant it. Thus, the employee has responded to a tense situation by becoming aware of his unconscious emotions and by controlling their influence over his rational behavior. He states his position, and the resulting intellectual catharsis allows his physical response to run down. His body returns to normal functioning.

As we see from this example, the combination of anger and fear is more likely to lead to catharsis than either emotion experienced alone. This is due, at least in part, to the fact that the biochemical outputs of the sympathetic and parasympathetic nervous systems in effect balance each other, enabling the body to quickly return to homeostasis.

The Destructiveness of Guilt

Guilt can be the most destructive emotional imbalance of all, and also the most irrational. Once a person is sensitized to react with feelings of guilt, shame, and self-blame, everything that goes wrong is accepted as a personal responsibility, with the statement, "It's all my fault."

The case of Susan demonstrates dramatically just how pervasive and destructive such a guilt orientation can be. Susan was severely and chronically depressed, to the point where she could barely function. In Selective Awareness, she immediately oriented back 17 years to the death of her younger brother, Lenny, for which she felt responsible. Lenny had been hit by a truck while they were playing ball in the street and had died as she held him. Not only did Susan blame herself for his death, she assumed that her parents and her older brother and younger sister blamed her also. She therefore cut herself off completely from the possibility of receiving their love and sympathy. In effect, she became the family slave, always doing things for other family members but never allowing them to give her anything in return.

While she was in high school, her father became ill with emphysema and was no longer able to work. She nursed him until he died and again blamed herself — if she had taken better care of him, he might not have died. At the age of 18, Susan assumed financial responsibility for herself, her mother, and her younger sister. When I first met her, she was 29 and still living with and supporting her mother. By this time, her feelings of guilt and depression were so overwhelming that she was afraid of losing her job.

As she continued to get in touch with her guilt and fear in Selective Awareness Therapy, Susan also began to recognize the anger she felt — at herself and at her family for accepting the role she had constructed for herself. And with the recognition of her own anger came the first relief from the guilt that had imprisoned her for years.

Susan made several tapes for herself in which she rehearsed the image of self-assertion. She rehearsed her image of herself in relation to her mother and to her older brother and younger sister, stressing the positive aspects of their relationship and her own feelings of self-confidence and self-worth. Soon she was able to give up her role as the "family slave."

Her change in attitude toward herself was so dramatic that before long she was receiving positive feedback from her friends and family. As she gave up her excessively humble, slave-like attitude, she became more acceptable to them. She moved into an apartment of her own and enjoyed closer family relationships than she had ever had before.

Although her progress was rapid, Susan had occasional setbacks. These relapses were useful in pointing out areas she had not yet dealt with. In evaluating one of these depressions, she found that she had several "automatic behaviors" that immediately made her assume responsibility for the welfare of her family. Since she also felt at times that her new lifestyle was risky, she made several image rehearsal tapes for risk-taking.

Last year at Christmas, a time she had only recently learned to enjoy, I received a letter from Susan. She wrote:

> Without the help of Selective Awareness, I would never have known life without the need to suffer. It is so great not only for me but certainly a lot easier on everyone else too . . . Living like this is so great! . . . This change does not come easily and still calls for a lot of work on my part, but thanks to the new understanding I have of myself, everyone else seems to feel better too. I even put a **"MY BEST FRIEND"** sign up on my mirror. How's that for progress?

Four

Bridging the Gap Between Mind and Body for Better Health

We know that some Indian fakirs are able to lie on a bed of nails; we know that in some cultures people can walk across red- hot coals without burning their feet. How do they do it? There is nothing different anatomically about their feet — except that theirs don't burn. These people have learned to influence their tissues to such a degree that they are able to limit the effects of the environment on their bodies.

Psychosomatic Behavior

Selective Awareness Therapy makes no distinction between mind and body, between psyche and soma. It bridges the gap between psychology and psychiatry on one hand and medicine on the other. With Selective Awareness Therapy you can learn to influence the functions of the autonomic nervous system that are involved in the disease process — including psychosomatic illness. *Psychosomatic* simply means that mind and body are one, and what affects one affects the other. As we have seen, fear, "nerves," worry, and anger can cause physical symptoms.

When emotions such as fear or anger are expressed fully, either through being acted out or through understanding and conscious control, the body returns to a state of homeostasis.

This release of emotional tension is called "catharsis." When an emotion is not fully expressed it may become chronic, and the symptoms caused by the biochemical component of the emotion may become chronic in the body. This relationship of thoughts and emotions within the body is called "somatization."

The relationship between emotions and bodily functions is demonstrated by the numerous disorders of the digestive system. Even our language reflects this relationship, in such expressions as, "I have to chew on it," "I can't swallow it," "I can't stomach that," and "Tight-assed." The stomach, colon, large intestine, and anus are all influenced by the ANS. When the consequences of the awareness or expression of emotion are too grim, repression occurs, causing diseases like spastic colitis, in which the sphincter goes into spasm; chronic diarrhea and constipation result.

When a person eats, he exhibits normal psychosomatic behavior. His choice of food is dictated by his psyche — in this case, his ability to discriminate what he should eat, how much, when, and where. The soma, responding accordingly, digests the food. If the choice was wrong, the body may rebel with a stomach ache or diarrhea. These symptoms are a normal signal for attention, transmitted by way of the ANS. But if the message is suppressed by the CNS, or if the response to the message is consciously or unconsciously resisted, psychosomatic disorder may occur. Thus, failure to return to health after a physical illness may be caused by a blockage of the self-corrective potential.

A person's physical appearance often reveals the emotions locked in his body. The overweight person, for example, suffers from over-absorption of food by the intestines; he is holding onto everything he can take in. In the underweight person, there is under-absorption by the intestines. The underweight person is trying to repel everything he takes in.

Influence Over Tissue Reaction

The case of Tom is a dramatic example of control over the "automatic" functions of the body through Selective Awareness.

Tom, a participant in a research project, had already achieved a high degree of influence over the functions of his autonomic nervous system through Selective Awareness. He therefore volunteered for the following experiment. He agreed to allow himself to be burned on the forearm after his finger signaled in Selective Awareness that it would be unnecessary to feel pain or to exhibit any other burn symptoms, such as blisters.

While Tom was in a state of Selective Awareness, with his eyes closed, his left forearm was burned with a cigarette. He experienced neither pain nor blistering, then or later.

Tom then agreed to allow his right arm to be burned. Again, he closed his eyes; again, he felt no pain. But this time, he allowed a blister to form. Instead of using a lit cigarette, however, the researcher placed an extinguished one against Tom's right forearm. Tom was deceived into believing that he had actually been burned. Within two hours, he did indeed have a blister, with surrounding irritation, although he had not been burned. His left arm failed to show any signs of having been burned, except for a touch of redness.

This experiment is important for at least two reasons. It shows the tremendous potential influence the individual can have over injury to the body. It also points out another important fact: an "imagined" injury can present all the physical symptoms of a "real" injury. The evidence of this experiment supports the theory that if a person imagines an injury from some source and creates an expectancy of illness, he may indeed receive that injury or illness.

Iatrogenic Communication

Iatrogenic disorders are also a reflection of the interaction of mind and body. "Iatrogenic" is defined, in Taber's *Cyclopedic Medical Dictionary*, as "an abnormal mental or physical condition induced in a patient by effects of treatment by a physician or surgeon. [The] term implies that such effects could have been avoided by proper and judicious care on the part of the physician." Iatrogenic communications, of course, may also involve paramedical personnel, ambulance drivers, nurses, or any other person dealing with patient care. The iatrogenic contribution may be as simple as a careless remark overheard or the patient's misinterpretation of the doctor's comments. It is frequently the case that what has been said and what a person has heard are two different things.

Expectations or assumptions that recovery from illness or accident will be slow or difficult may actually slow down or stop the self-corrective process. As in the following case, iatrogenic communication can cause a limited and pessimistic outlook for the recovery of health.

Throwing Out the Garbage

Sally was 28 years old when I first saw her as a patient. Four years earlier she had broken her hip in falling off a boulder while on a fishing trip. She spent two months in the hospital, but even after her release she did not improve. The pain in her hip, at first bearable, grew worse and worse until she was almost totally disabled. When we began Selective Awareness Therapy, the first things revealed were several severe iatrogenic communications.

The trouble began when the ambulance driver who took her to the hospital told her, "You have a very bad break, the way that leg is twisted." When she arrived at the hospital, her own physician said, "This is the worst hip fracture I have ever seen." She also vividly recalled having picked up negative information while under sedation, when she heard a discussion between her family doctor and an orthopedic surgeon about the possibility of her fracture not healing at all and requiring a prosthetic device.

When Sally realized in Selective Awareness Therapy how all the strongly negative input she had received had prevented her hip fracture from healing, she decided to change the situation. After all, her own mind had kept her leg from healing properly; therefore she could use the same power to be able to walk normally again. As her interest in self-healing grew, she developed an enthusiastic "let's show them" attitude. First, in Selective Awareness, she constructed a mental "garbage pail," into which she tossed all of the iatrogenic communications she had heard and overheard. Then I explained to her the dynamics of the healing of fractures: the laying of fibrous tissue, calcification, the reforming of cartilage. She checked out library books on anatomy and physiology. When she fully understood *how* her leg should heal, she made a series of image rehearsal tapes and played them daily. Her improvement from then on was dramatic. Soon she was able to get out of her walker, and within a few months dispensed with her cane. The following letter, which she kindly agreed to allow me to print, shows that the process of healing continued far beyond the original expectations of her doctors.

Dear Doctor!

I get better each year. It has been ten years this June since the fishing accident when I broke my femur, and about eight years when Dr. Smith told me to have the prosthesis. I am sure grateful to you for giving me help.

We have an acre out here and I do all my housework plus a lot of gardening, and I have a twelve-year-old boy and a husband to cook for. My mother is at present living in the guest house. So all in all I am so grateful to get around without a cane or anything. I do limp a bit and would not do so much of that if all my shoes had a half inch added to the sole. If I walk all day or garden all day I feel it, so I let up and do a bit of sewing.

Dr. Brown did say I was doing so well with my hip

that I should not have anything done to it until I had to. Said when I went on long jaunts to use a cane. Haven't done that for years.

Thank you.

Sincerely,

Sally

Symptom-Producing Events and Tissue Memory

Before going on to the next Selective Awareness exercise, we need to be familiar with a few more terms, such as "Symptom-Producing Event," "Tissue Memory," and "Amnestic Learning." These terms and concepts are actually tools with which to work in Selective Awareness; understanding why and how symptoms are produced is not only important in working with these symptoms but can be very therapeutic in itself.

As we learned earlier, for every thought-emotion there is a corresponding physical or psychological symptom, whether conscious or subconscious. These physical or psychological symptoms are the result of unresolved thought-emotion complexes. And for every physical symptom, the reverse is true — rarely can a physical symptom exist for an extended period of time without changing the way the individual thinks and feels. The purpose of Selective Awareness Therapy is to establish a link between the two, in order to resolve the thought-emotion-physical symptom complex and influence the mind and body to a state of healthy homeostasis. That change may involve controlling ANS functions as well as influencing the self-image to accept positive change and new behavior patterns.

When the homeostatic mechanism is disturbed by physical injury or by an unresolved thought-emotion-physical symptom complex, scars of relative permanence may result that do not permit the return to homeostatic balance. Injury and scarring may occur on a psychological level or a physical level. It is also possible to receive an injury on a psycho-physiological level —

that is, an injury to the body combined with a very strong emotion. That is how "tissue memory" is created.

When a physical injury to the body is accompanied by a strong emotion, that part of the body may become sensitized and react strongly to future emotional states. The head, neck, and back are particularly vulnerable to this kind of sensitization. Tissue memory is always a component of chronic muscular pain. Organs too may be sensitized in the presence of emotion — as we have seen, the stomach and digestive system are frequently affected by emotional stress.

Even if an injury is incurred strictly on a physical level it may leave tissue memory. This tissue memory, created at the time of the sensitizing event, may cause only occasional malfunction, which the self-corrective potential will return to normal. But when a number of injuries occur on different physiological levels at the same time as a major physical crisis, the coping mechanism may collapse and produce persistent ill health.

While an emotional state may stimulate the sensitivity of a tissue memory and produce a symptom, it is also true that tissue memory alone may be responsible for the occurrence of symptoms that may produce a particular physical or emotional response.

The theory of tissue memory rests on the assumption that at any time in life, including the birth process itself, a tissue may be injured in the presence of a prevailing emotion, producing both tissue memory and emotional memory, conscious or subconscious. The result is that the affected organ responds strongly during future symptom-producing events.

When the tissue memory is considered with the subconscious and conscious memory of the traumatizing event (symptom-producing event), the thought-emotion-tissue response becomes an overwhelming negative influence for the body.

Of course, sensitization also happens on a purely physical level. Cannon's Law[1] states that when an organ or muscle is injured or destroyed, the affected structure develops an in-

---

[1] "A Law of Denervation," in *Am. J. of Sci.*, 98:737-750, 1939.

creased sensitivity to the biochemical agents released by the CNS and ANS in response to the accompanying emotional state.

According to the theory of tissue memory, even the skeletal muscles, usually controlled by the central nervous system, are influenced by the autonomic nervous system at times of physical injury with accompanying emotional stress. In that way sensitization produces tissue memory, meaning that the physical symptoms will be reproduced in response to the same emotion in the future. Both psychological sensitization and physiological symptoms work together as a result of the unresolved emotions. The snowballing effect of this sensitization may lead to a cumulative overload of the homeostatic mechanism, resulting in an imbalance in the system. Accompanying messages are interpreted by the brain as being of a very serious nature, and a "nervous breakdown" with physical collapse may be pending.

Selective Awareness Therapy allows you to review the symptom-producing events that originally caused the malfunction. It allows you to recognize the ways in which a return to homeostasis, or balance, is made difficult or impossible by the creation of physical and emotional energy blocks. In cases where the thought-emotion-physical symptom complex is easily recognized and corrected, the improvement will be immediate. In cases where the sensitizing events are obscure because there is no conscious memory of them, more time and practice may be needed.

Once you understand the whole chain of symptom-producing events and sensitizing events, you can review and update those assumptions and values that may be causing trouble. But remember that just as ill health can be brought on or extended by subconscious factors, the return to health can be, too. The mind-body system gets sick without your conscious understanding of all the causative factors. Fortunately, when the self-corrective potential is unblocked, it can teach the body to heal itself in the same way. Therefore it's not really necessary to track down every symptom-producing event, or to go all the way back to the symptom-sensitizing event, to attain the state of homeostatic balance and mind-body harmony.

Healing an Injured Back

The case history of Natalie demonstrates how tissue memory can actually prevent normal healing.

Natalie's car had been rear-ended while she was stopped for a red light. She had felt a sudden sharp pain in her lower back and in the back of her neck. She was taken to the hospital and was treated with heat, physical therapy, and pain medication. When her condition did not improve, she was put in a back cast; she had to stay in bed for six weeks. During this period, she developed rheumatoid arthritis in her hands. Despite all the treatment she received, her condition continued to deteriorate, and by the time I met her she was totally disabled. She was very depressed about her condition and felt completely hopeless. Her social life was almost nonexistent, and her career as an actress was at a complete standstill.

In Selective Awareness, Natalie quickly oriented back to the time of her accident. She reported feeling overwhelming anger. She had just signed a contract for a part in a play that would be very important to her career, and as the other car struck her from behind she felt an explosion of tremendous anger and a flash of realization that she would have to go to the hospital and would probably be in bed for some time. This anger, combined with her physical injury, created tissue memory. Throughout her conventional therapy, this tissue memory kept her from getting well. She also experienced great anger at herself and at her body because of her failure to improve.

Once she understood the dynamics of her symptoms and the way that tissue memory had prevented her from recuperating, Natalie recovered dramatically. After three sessions in Selective Awareness, the pain was gone from her hands and neck, although her lower back was still sore. She was able to resume an active social life and return to work.

After a few weeks, however, the pain began to return, threatening to cripple her once again. In Selective Awareness, she quickly determined that her anger had returned — now she was furious with herself for having been bed-ridden for eighteen months when it had proved so easy to cure herself in only three Selective Awareness sessions. Image rehearsal, working with anger and self-blame, soon cleared up the problem.

Interestingly, Natalie did retain a small area of tenderness in her lower back which acted as a barometer of her emotional and physical state. If her anger returned, or if she worked too hard, the pain would flare up as a signal that her attention was required. This recurrence of symptoms is common when dramatic recovery from a long-term illness occurs. I refer to this as a face-saving device caused by guilt feelings for having been ill for such a long time, or sick at all, and then being cured as if by magic.

Curing the Persistent Headache

In addition to demonstrating how tissue memory works, the following case history illustrates many of the other elements discussed in the previous sections.

Although this case history is condensed, the events described really did take place in just one session of Selective Awareness Therapy. While you are reading it, please remember that the system of "consider, consult, consent" was used every step of the way. John's permission was obtained, through the use of ideomotor finger signals, before he responded to any questions.

John, a 45-year-old businessman, had been suffering daily headaches for six years, ever since an automobile accident in which he flipped end-over-end several times and was knocked unconscious. His two children, who were also in the car, were not seriously hurt. John remained unconscious for almost two days, followed by six weeks in the hospital, during which time he was treated with physiotherapy and medication, including muscle relaxants. From the moment he regained consciousness, he suffered severe headaches. After several months of treatment, during which he found no relief from his headaches, further tests were performed and a ruptured cervical disc was found. But after surgical removal of the disc, John's headaches did not improve. Two months later another disc was removed. Still the headaches persisted, and this time treatment consisted of cervical traction, hot packs, muscle relaxants, and pain medication.

Eventually yet a third disc was removed, his neck was fused, and this time John was placed in a body cast. He still had his headaches, but was told that they would be relieved in a few days, or certainly upon removal of the cast. When six weeks had passed after the cast was off and he still had headaches, he was referred to me for consultation and Selective Awareness Therapy.

On his first visit, John oriented back almost immediately to his most recent headache-producing experience. When his "Yes" finger signaled his consent, he was asked to describe, "Where are you, what's going on, how do you feel?" He stated that he was going over the books for his company, which was in trouble because of his lengthy illness and huge medical expenses, and that he was worried and afraid. He was then asked to go back to another symptom-producing event, to another day when he had a headache. Again his concerns were of a financial nature, regarding his business. He stated that he was afraid of going bankrupt.

Although John connected the onset of his headaches to his car accident at age 39, he was asked to go back to a time earlier in his life when he had a headache, and he immediately remembered a time in his early teens when he felt fear and anxiety over a math exam for which he was ill-prepared. He had a severe headache at that time.

In seeking the primary sensitizing event which taught him the habit of ill health, I asked John to orient back to a time when he was approximately ten years old, to a scene of his choice.

He stated that he was having a good time at a fair and described his clothes and the scenery vividly. Again he had a headache, and his finger signals indicated that he was able to identify the emotion he was experiencing as anxiety. It seems that he had deliberately wandered away from his parents in the crowd, in order to do what *he* wanted to do at the fair, and had been unable to find them for some time.

He was then asked to orient back to age eight and again described a scene where he was ill with a headache. Again he was very specific about all the circumstances — the clothes he wore, the room he was in, the other people present. Again the prevalent emotion was anxiety.

Orienting back to age five, John described a scene in which he was visiting his aunt and uncle. They took him boating and he remembered feeding the ducks. When asked if this little boy, age five, knew what it was like to have a headache, he signaled "No" with his "No" finger. It was obvious that something had happened between ages five and eight that had taught this youngster to have headaches. He was then asked to let himself come up from age five to the first time he was aware that he had a headache. He flashed on that event suddenly and appeared very startled. His voice was that of a little boy as he described the following incident: "I am six years old, I am playing in my backyard with my father's puppies." He had been told not to play with his father's puppies because they were valuable. During his play, he accidentally dropped and killed one of the puppies. This was early in the morning and he had all day to worry about it, until by the afternoon he ended up with a headache. His worries were justified, and he was severely punished.

Every event elicited so far contained either fear or a variation of fear, such as worry or concern. He was then asked to review what had happened at the time of his accident, when his car flipped end-over-end and he was knocked unconscious. He remembered very little, not only of the car accident but of the entire day preceding the accident — a common condition called retrograde amnesia. But suddenly he recalled vividly what had happened and as he saw himself rolling over and over in the car, he shouted, "Oh my God, what is happening to the kids in the back of the car." Then he was knocked unconscious, to awaken two days later.

It seemed very obvious that through the process of tissue memory, John had learned to associate headaches with fear, and with any variations on the theme of fear. He was then asked if in the light of his newly gained insight he still needed to have headaches in the presence of fear, to which he signaled "No." He was then asked to go through all of the events he had reported before with image rehearsal, this time seeing himself without the accompanying headache. Each time he successfully completed an image rehearsal he indicated his accomplishment with a "Yes" signal. This image rehearsal included the primary sensitizing event at age six when he accidentally killed one of his father's puppies.

In order to further desensitize himself against the headaches that accompanied fear, John was asked to imagine future events when he would be able to handle anxiety-producing situations without headaches. John's headaches cleared up, and in the several years since then he has never had a crippling headache, but only a few minor ones that he has been able to work out immediately through Selective Awareness.

Using Age Regression to Discover Symptom-Producing Events

I didn't really meet Richard S. until I attended his wedding, but I think his case history illustrates a couple of important points. First, it shows clearly the process of orienting back to symptom-producing events and working with that material. And second, it demonstrates how effective Selective Awareness Therapy can be in self-healing without the aid of a therapist. In fact, it was Richard's report of his own experience with Selective Awareness Therapy, and others like his, that gave me the idea of writing a book about the process of self-help and self-healing.

When I received a thick manila envelope in the mail one day, I didn't recognize the name or the return address. But the contents were very exciting. It was a long letter from Richard S., who had attended a two-day seminar I had given on Selective Awareness Therapy at a university. The seminar had been intended to train professional therapists in the use of Selective Awareness, but Richard had decided to try the techniques on himself. He was so pleased with the results that he wrote up his personal history notes as a report, and sent them to me. Here are some excerpts from his report.

Symptoms: Stomach cramps, alternating diarrhea and constipation. Also severe, incapacitating headaches, mostly upon arising, located frontally above the eyes, with tightness in the neck.

Medical History Review: These complaints have been evaluated by upper G.I. barium X-rays and barium enema sigmoidoscopy, and a general physical examination — all results negative.

In my *first session* I reacquainted myself with the state of Selective Awareness and the ideomotor finger signals. I started the session with a headache, which had notably subsided by the end of the session.

Second session: Oriented back to the last time I had a bad stomachache. Saw myself clearly at a staff meeting two weeks ago when I was passed over for promotion in favor of a good friend of mine. This was a real double-bind situation because I was glad he got the promotion, but I wanted it myself. As soon as I recognized that I was angry I felt guilty. And then I felt a great deal of relief just from becoming aware of having been caught in that double bind. The stomachache I'd had for two weeks was cleared up by the end of the session.

(A double-bind situation exists when you are "damned if you do — damned if you don't." Richard was "damned" if he became angry, "damned" if he didn't get angry and express his feelings.)

Third session: Exploring the nature of my headaches. Orienting back to the first symptom-producing event, I saw myself asking a girl for a date to go to a high school party. She turned me down, and I experienced the emotions of fear and rejection. I then allowed myself to be drawn further and further back in time by what first appeared to be a headache and ended up being a very strong, painful pulling sensation. To my surprise I appeared to be going through the birth process. I experienced mostly fear and pain and immediately returned to the state of Social Awareness. I didn't want to stay there and go through the birth process, but it really gave me something to think about.

Fourth session: Still on headaches. Oriented back to a fight with my older brother who was screaming at me, "You scrawny piggy." I remember he used to call me that a lot. Emotions: Fear, anger, a feeling of rejection.

Another incident — the little girl next door is the same age as I am — we're both six — but she's bigger and heavier than I am, and she's teasing me and daring me to fight. She throws a tomato and hits me in the face. I run in the house.

Age eleven — my older sister has a girlfriend over to spend the night and I feel very uncomfortable about having this strange girl in the house. Emotions: embarrassment, fear, possibly rejection.

Age seventeen — I stay away from the beach all summer because a girl told me I was skinny.

Richard's full report was 56 typewritten pages — too long to be reproduced here. In summary, he became aware for the first time just how sensitive he was about his small stature and slight build, and how this sensitivity, along with his fear of rejection, had made it impossible for him to establish any but the most superficial relationship with a woman. Almost all of his symptom-producing events had to do with anger, fear, and rejection — usually rejection by a woman.

Once he had become familiar with the emotional basis for his stomach problems and headaches (which had cleared up spontaneously by this time), Richard made himself several tapes in which he reviewed all of the symptom-producing events that had come up, from the aggressive little girl at the age of six to the staff meeting at which he was passed over for promotion. (He decided to stay away from reviewing the birth process.) As he reviewed each of these events he rehearsed a positive image of himself, replacing fear and anger and rejection with self- assurance and confidence in his ability to handle any situation. As he wrote, "I found out that most of those situations that caused me so much pain were really just child's play. Kids can be cruel, but I took it all to heart and made it a part of myself."

Richard also imagined several arbitrary future situations in which he performed with ease and confidence, seeing himself as he had always wanted to be. He imagined himself presenting a report at a staff meeting, and he imagined himself meeting women and not feeling shy or awkward or overcome by fear or rejection. About that time he noticed that he was beginning to put on weight for the first time in his life — apparently his body had gotten the message. He enrolled in a tennis class, the first time he had ever attempted a sport, and found that his small size was actually an advantage, for he was light and quick on his feet.

Richard's report is an excellent example of the need to deal with one problem at a time, in the order of priority. As he dealt with each problem, he also improved his self-image.

I wrote to Richard, thanking him for taking the trouble to send me the report on his Selective Awareness Therapy, and we corresponded for about a year. Then I received the invitation to his wedding. When we finally met, it was as though we were already old friends.

Amnestic Learning

As we have seen, the state of Selective Awareness is reached by the reduction of cortical activity through progressive relaxation and pleasant imagery. By reducing cortical activity it is possible to "bypass the critical factor," thus stopping the self-evaluative, judgmental, and self-appraisal processes of the brain. Response to external stimuli is reduced, leading to an increased awareness of internal psycho-physiological phenomena — what's going on in your mind and body. This selective awareness can be directed toward emotions, thought-emotions, and thought-emotion-physical symptom complexes. This awareness is so increased and specific that it may break through the "amnestic barrier." Amnestic learning is what we learned before we were aware of the learning process. Thus it is possible to reach into memories that extend all the way back to birth and to update them with adult insight.

The brain is always recording its learning experiences; these recordings can be decoded even though they were made before we learned to understand symbols and language. To understand amnestic learning, it is best to view the human self-system from the moment of conception. With the egg's fertilization by the sperm, the fetus begins a totally dependent existence, taking from the mother the nourishment it needs for its own development and survival. In the uterus, the fetus is totally dependent on the mother via the placenta. It develops its own heartbeat and yet exchanges blood with the mother. The placenta is permeable to all vitamins and nutrients, including the mother's biochemical reaction to emotions in states of fear, worry, and anger. "Growing up" in such an atmosphere may shape the reality of the newborn.

The brain has developed by birth and is capable of learning by imprinting. At birth, the infant moves toward independence when the umbilical cord is severed. He establishes an independent breathing rhythm and self-life begins. However, he is still physically and socially dependent and soon learns the reality of frustration, reward, and punishment. Although unable to speak and understand, he begins to learn immediately, first through imprinting and conditioning and then through subconscious reasoning as well.

We learn more rapidly between the ages of zero and four than at any other time of life, and yet most of us have no memory of those important years, except perhaps as occasional glimpses. But, like the hidden part that supports the visible tip of the iceberg, this learned material is the basis of all our adult values and beliefs. What we learned as infants still has a profound effect on us as adults — on the decisions we make or don't make, the way we live our lives and relate to other people, our self-image, and our state of health. Some of the material that is dealt with in Selective Awareness Therapy is composed of such early assumptions. In order to work with them, we must investigate how they were formed.

How is it possible to remember events all the way back to birth, before you were able to speak or to understand what was being said around and to you? The brain is perfectly formed at birth, and even before birth it is making recordings. Some of these, particularly if they're "taped" in the presence of fear, make a fairly deep impression on the mind. It's a big advantage to have an adult viewpoint in going after these early memories because a lot of the things that happened then will be distorted in memory — if only because you were just two feet tall and couldn't understand what was going on. Can you imagine, for example, being confronted by a barking dog taller than you are? That could be frightening, especially if you lack the experience to understand that the dog is just being friendly and playful.

With Selective Awareness Therapy you can go back to the amnestic learning period and get an idea of your own development in terms of self-image and self-esteem. Remember that when you enter the state of Selective Awareness you're conscious — super-conscious, in fact, and able to deal with the hidden assumptions that have escaped you before.

In working on a particular symptom in Selective Awareness, you will find that age regression occurs almost automatically from one symptom-producing event to the next. Whether you are working with conscious memories or amnestic material, however, it is important to remember the system of consider, consult, consent. "Is it all right to remember an event at age eight?" "Would it be OK to let that symptom go?" And if your finger signals "No," respect that response. There's always plenty of other material to work with, and usually this resistance will vanish after a couple of sessions. Remember, in Selective Awareness Therapy there is no need to force anything that doesn't come easily.

How to Deal with Resistance

The case history of "Mrs. Alice" illustrates how it is possible to work with these "No" signals when for some reason it seems necessary to hang onto a symptom, or at least a part of one.

Mrs. Alice, a lady in her late seventies, was referred to me with herpes pain syndrome — that is, pain following shingles. She had been suffering this severe pain for over seven years. The location of the pain, typical of shingles, was slightly above the belt on one side just at the end of the rib cage. She told me that the pain was so severe that she could not stand the touch of clothes against her skin. As a result, she wore only flimsy gowns and had seldom been out of her house for seven years.

This was relatively early in my experience with Selective Awareness Therapy, and I tried every approach I could think of to get this woman to give up her pain. But every time I asked "Would it be all right to let go of the pain," her "No" finger would begin signaling wildly. I was ready to throw in the towel, but she said, "Young man, if you don't mind, I would like to continue seeing you."

So we proceeded for a few more sessions until one day I had a brilliant idea — while Mrs. Alice was in Selective Awareness I asked her if it would be all right to give up the pain, to which she signaled "No." I then asked her if it would be all right for her to keep the pain but not to have it hurt anymore — to which she signaled "Yes"!

This was the end of Mrs. Alice's pain; she was able to dress and leave the house, in which she'd been a prisoner for so long. For whatever reason, she was able to "have her cake and eat it too." She was able to retain her pain, but it no longer hurt.

Reviewing Birth without Having to Relive It

Carol

Another history, that of Carol, illustrates both an organ-sensitizing event leading to tissue memory and another method of working with a negative response via the ideomotor finger signals.

Carol was a woman of 22 who experienced violent head-aches, accompanied by anxiety and fear. As we traced her symptom- producing events backward in age she became more and more anxious, until at age 3 she became quite fidgety and restless, and her hands were cold and sweaty. I asked her if she would like to go back to her birth to see if this might be a birth-connected sensitization. She nodded her head and said "Yes," but her "No" finger came up. I asked her if she knew what it was like to have a headache at age three. This time her "Yes" finger came up, but she shook her head — meaning, "Yes, I know what happened, but I don't want to have anything to do with it."

Again I asked, "Would you like to go back and see what it's like to be born?" She nodded her head in agreement, but her "No" finger came up.

I then asked, "Would it be all right for you to see on a television screen what's happening?" to which her "Yes" finger agreed. I asked her to visualize a television screen on which the birth of a child would be portrayed and to let her "Yes" finger signal when she could see the screen. Soon it began to signal. She was keenly interested in what was going on, and began to describe what she was seeing. "I see a baby and it's hanging upside down." She described a dual feeling of "Yes — this is me, but it's out there" and stated that the experience was not painful for her to go through. Her description was clear and detailed: as the baby was being born, the cord wrapped around her neck and she was asphyxiated. She was delivered by forceps. After about two hours of intensive work to resuscitate her, she was put in an incubator in the intensive care unit.

The scene Carol described was very detailed — she saw the masks on the faces of the doctors and nurses, the lights of the operating room, the surgical instruments on the tray.

Carol called her mother in my presence. Her mother was surprised to hear that Carol had learned what had happened to her at birth because, as she said, "We never told you. How did you find out?"

Carol's comment was that she was very grateful to understand the origin of her headaches, and she also felt grateful that she didn't have to live through the experience of strangling at birth again in Selective Awareness, but only to watch it happening on a television screen.

This case clearly demonstrates the necessity of dealing with yourself carefully, and using consider, consult, consent every step of the way, especially in working with early childhood experiences. Obviously, it's possible to learn a great deal by reviewing the birth experience. In Selective Awareness, however, there's no need to relive birth or any other painful experience — you've already lived through it once. Anything you need to know, including information about your emotional state, can be gathered from simple observation and review in the state of Selective Awareness.

Gloria

The following report, which illustrates the ability to recall very early amnestic material in the state of Selective Awareness, was prepared by Gloria, a graduate student in psychology at the university where I teach. This case history shows once again the necessity for very careful handling of such material.

First Session

I arrived at class with what I call a "blazing headache" — extreme photosensitivity coupled with a throbbing head. My only desire was to curl up on the rug and sleep. The headache had begun in the morning and increased in intensity during the day. I had decided to volunteer myself as a patient at the class simply in hopes of defusing this headache. I'd always felt that my headaches were directly related to my emotional state but had not been able to short-circuit them. Aspirin was completely useless.

Sandra (a fellow student) acted as my therapist. I felt very withdrawn and cut off as though my headache were acting as a kind of fence. The lights in the classroom bothered me a great deal and were dimmed. In response to Sandra's questions, via my ideomotor finger signals, we determined that I knew what it was like to have a headache prenatally. When told to go to a time before my first headache, I swung away from the one remaining light in the room, realized that there were no words where I was, and verbalized this. My heart was pounding. I felt great curiosity and a kind of terror.

Dr. Mutke had me open my eyes and asked if it was OK for him to take over as therapist. I said, "OK." He said, "We have a heavy one here," and I laughed. Closing my eyes, I returned to the place where I had been with Sandra as my therapist. Dr. Mutke asked me to describe what I was seeing.

The next part of this report is taken from the tape recording that Sandra made during that session.

GLORIA: I am resisting.
DR. MUTKE: Why are you resisting?

G: I don't believe what I'm seeing.

M: Describe what you are seeing.

G: It looks like an operating room, full of people. So much light, bloody pink light.

M: Describe the people.

G: They are all wearing white or maybe the bright light makes it look white.

M: What's on the clothing?

G: There's blood all over their gowns.

M: What else do you see?

G: A body, a very white body lying there. There's blood on that white body. The light makes the body look so white.

M: Who is that?

G: I guess that's my mother and she's cut open.

M: That's an episiotomy. They're normal. Can you accept that they're normal and nothing to be afraid of?[2]

G: [My "Yes" finger responded.]

M: Go back to the time before this incident, describe what's going on.

G: [Again there are no words, everything is dark and nice. Suddenly I feel that I am being forced upward. Curiosity and panic.] There is some sort of activity going on above me. Drawn up.

M: What's happening?

G: [Yelling] That stupid son-of-a-bitch pulled me up by my head!

M: What was that?

G: That bastard pulled me up by my head like that. [Indicating pressure under jaws and along the side of the head.]

M: What's going on now?

G: I guess I'm born and I don't like it.

M: Look around — what do you see?

G: Those people in the bloody white gowns.

M: Open your eyes and tell me what you are seeing.

---

[2] This was a mistaken assumption on my part. I did not know at the time that Gloria had been delivered by Cesarean section, only that forceps had been used.

G: At first all I saw were my classmates, although I only focused on those wearing white. Gradually the operating room came into focus again. [The rest of the session must have taken place with my eyes open.]

M: What's happening?

G: I guess I'm being held and looking down at my mother. I'm still mad. [I felt as though I was looking through something, perhaps a film of some sort on my eyes.]

M: Does it feel good to he held?

G: No, I'm messy and I'm naked — exposed.

M: What's the next thing you see?

G: I'm in a glass crib, the nursery I guess.

M: And then?

G: Oh, the nurse is taking me to my mother. She's so happy. She's smiling and saying "My pretty baby." She's really glad to have me.

M: Do you feel now that it was worth it to go through what you did to be born?

G: Yeah, I guess so, she's so happy.

M: Would you like to re-experience the first time you experienced nursing?

G: [My "Yes" finger responded.]

M: How does it feel?

G: Good, soothing. [Feelings of all-encompassing warmth and satisfaction.]

M: Would you like to show everyone how good it feels to be nursing?

G: No, I'm a shy baby.

The remainder of the session was devoted to accepting the fact that as painful as the birth experience was, I had, after all, "made it" and it was probably worth it. Responding to Peter's questions and statements, I "let go" of those ancient, negative feelings.

Returning to Social Awareness, I was completely relaxed, smiling, without a hint of the headache that had had me cringing an hour before. Even the lights in the room didn't affect me. My "up-tight" back muscles, which had been rigid before the session, were fluid. My shoulders felt as though they positively drooped — it was wonderful. It was glorious to reclaim a "lost" part of myself. Perhaps the best part of all was to have re-experienced my mother's unbounded love for me, her long-awaited firstborn.

Second Session

Reporting on my "headache status" since the first session, almost four weeks earlier. Since that first session I have not had a single headache. For me, someone who has had extensive, intense headaches for as long as I can remember, this total lack of headaches is completely amazing. It's as though "headache" is simply no longer a part of my vocabulary. The very idea of having a headache is quite foreign to me now. I've washed my hands of them.

(Because headaches had always been such an intrinsic part of my "bad feelings," I feared a kind of symptom substitution resulting in increased eating. The second session dealt with these "loose ends.")

I had had frequent sessions with Selective Awareness by myself for four weeks. After the first therapy session, I gave great attention to the muscles of my back which seemed to be the trigger points for my headaches (or shall I say "former headaches"?) I also gave myself suggestions (as Dr. Mutke had done at the end of the first session) to have, remember, and understand important dreams and insights. My whole attitude was, "Zip, zap, the headaches are gone, now there are other things to deal with, especially my weight."

In Selective Awareness, I was able to let go of the idea that I had to have some kind of symptom substitution, that it was OK to simply be rid of the headaches. Dr. Mutke had me recall a situation which would normally "give me a headache." I disclosed a work situation and we reviewed it, looking for other ways to deal with it rather than producing a headache. (I thought about zapping an irate customer with a phaser gun *a la* "Star Trek," and giggled about this to myself.) I said that it would be better to expend energy digging a garden rather than getting a headache. I was having trouble attempting to deal with ways of avoiding headaches, since "headache" was such an outdated concept for me. I felt that headaches had been one way (long-standing, dramatic, and painful) for me to "sabotage" myself; now that they were gone, the next step was to deal with their "second cousin," my weight problem. Everything became perfectly clear as I moved from Selective Awareness to Social Awareness: the headaches and the weight problem were indeed the major ways in which I "sabotaged" myself, prevented myself from growing, from becoming what I can become.

I have arrived at a point in my life where my whole desire is to grow, to expand — but it's a scary business, not unlike standing on the edge of a great void. It's like the Chinese character for the word "Crisis": Danger and Opportunity. Somehow headaches and overeating are not desirable but they are old habits ("Old habits die hard") and in a way they are known and safe.

Five

Practicing Selective Awareness Therapy

The preceding case histories give a good idea of the process, direction, and scope of Selective Awareness Therapy. Although in each of these cases a therapist was present, all the tools you need are contained in this book. In general, when you begin to work on a symptom, such as a weight problem or recurrent back pain, you will follow a course similar to that shown in the examples.

In Selective Awareness you will orient back to a symptom-producing event and then work either forward or backward in time from that event, examining three or four events when that particular symptom was present. You can take a good look at each event and ask, "What's going on?" "Who's there?" "How do I feel, what is my emotional state?" What you're really after is the emotion and the thought-emotion complex that is tied in with the physical symptom. Sometimes it is possible to go all the way back to the original symptom-sensitizing event, and sometimes it isn't. Usually, it isn't even necessary at all.

One way of investigating a symptom is simply to go back to a time when you had that symptom badly — a particularly severe headache, for example. Recall the events that occurred on that particular day, see what was going on around you, and let yourself become aware of the accompanying emotion.

You might find that the emotion most frequently accompanying your headache is anger. And that anger might lead you to remember incidents in your childhood when you weren't allowed to express it. Or you might find that the main emotion you experience with a headache is fear. Then you might uncover the message, "Boys don't cry. Be a brave boy." Or, "Nice girls don't get angry."

Frequently, anger and fear work together to produce a symptom. After all, anger at parents and other authority figures frequently brings punishment. Or you may feel, "I'm doing something wrong, and I deserve to be punished," and then you feel guilty. And when you feel guilty, of course, you immediately look around for the punishment you know is coming, because our culture is oriented to the system of reward and punishment. If you are a good boy or good girl you are rewarded. If you're bad you stand in the corner or get whipped. Once you have identified your emotion or your thought-emotion content, then you have something to work with in image rehearsal.

It frequently happens that just the act of paying attention to yourself and your emotions in a relaxed, non-threatening environment, with the knowledge that you have the power to influence your own health, is enough to allow insight and relief of symptoms. As your attitudes and assumptions change, you may find that patterns of ill health in your life suddenly become clear and begin to change.

And you will also find that the more you practice Selective Awareness the more in touch you become with all your emotions — not just fear and anger but love and joy as well.

Summary

When you decide to investigate the origin of a physical symptom, there are several steps to be followed.

Write It Down

In your Personal History notebook write down everything that comes to mind about that symptom — when you first remember experiencing it, under what circumstances it is most likely to occur, whether or not it is usually accompanied by a particular emotional state that you are aware of. If you have seen a doctor about this condition, include a medical history review. Finally, write down exactly what it is that you want to investigate.

Go into the State of Selective Awareness

Simply count back from ten to one, using whatever words and images are appropriate for you or make a tape of your favorite induction. Check with your ideomotor finger signals to see that you are deeply relaxed and comfortable in the state of Selective Awareness. (If anything comes up that you want to investigate while you are doing another exercise in this book, simply shut off the tape recorder and follow the rest of the process outlined here.)

Orient Back to Several Symptom-Producing Events

Ask yourself, "Is it all right to find out more about (whatever it is that you want to investigate)?" When your "Yes" finger signals affirmation, allow your mind to orient back to the last time you experienced the symptom. Where are you? What are you doing? Who are you with? And how do you feel? When the scene is clear and vivid in your mind, allow your "Yes" finger to lift. Now orient back to another symptom-producing event and follow the same procedure. Do this three or four times, until you become aware of a common thread running through all the symptom-producing events. Don't attempt to do too much in one session — remember that you can review this material as often as you wish and take two or three sessions to explore the same area if you wish.

Another method of review is to allow your mind to orient back to the *earliest* symptom-producing event, or symptom-sensitizing event, and then come forward in time from then. If you find yourself reviewing something like the birth process, or anything you don't care to review, simply return to the state of Social Awareness. And remember, there's no need to *relive* anything in the state of Selective Awareness — you've already lived through it once. You can simply observe and learn from the material you review. One helpful technique for maintaining objectivity is to imagine that you are viewing a television or movie screen, seeing yourself as though you are another person.

Search for the Common Thread

When you have reviewed three or four symptom-producing events, return to the state of Social Awareness and write down everything you have learned. Pay particular attention to the emotional state that is common to all the situations your mind has chosen for review. This is the "thought-emotion process," which is tied in with your physical symptom. The goal of Selective Awareness Therapy is to let you become aware of and to break that connection, to free the energy tied up in that thought-emotion-physical symptom complex, and to allow the mind- body system to return to a state of physical and emotional balance.

Image Rehearsal

When you understand the emotional component of the symptom- producing events you have reviewed, go back into the state of Selective Awareness. (You may want to do this right away, or you may want to let the information "jell" for a day or so. There's no hurry — the material will still be there when you're ready to return to it.) Allow your mind to orient back to the first symptom-producing event, and ask yourself, "Is it all right to let go of the pain and negative emotion in this situation?" When your "Yes" finger signals affirmation, review that symptom- producing event again — but this time see yourself functioning in a healthy, positive fashion, free of physical pain and painful emotions. When your "Yes" finger signals that this positive image is clear and vivid in your mind, allow yourself to orient back to the next symptom-producing event, and repeat the process.

If your "No" finger signals, "No, it's not all right to let go of that pain," respect that message from your inner mind. In that case, you can either drop that area of investigation for the moment and return to it later, or you can continue to investigate, to try to find out *why* it's not all right to let go of that particular pain or negative emotion just yet. But do be gentle with yourself, and remember to use the system of *consider, consult, and consent* every step of the way.

When you have completed your positive image rehearsal of the symptom-producing events, you will have a good idea of how it would feel to live in the world without that particular symptom. Now project yourself into the future, and imagine yourself in similar situations. See yourself as you would like to be, functioning calmly and with self-assurance, and with no need for physical symptoms or negative emotional reactions.

When you have completed your future image rehearsal, return to the state of Social Awareness. Once again, write down everything you have learned, paying particular attention to how you feel *now*.

Give Yourself Positive Feedback

As soon as you notice improvement in your physical symptom — which will probably be very soon — give yourself some positive feedback. In the state of Selective Awareness, review the progress you've made. Congratulate yourself, allow yourself to feel pride in your ability to use Selective Awareness to take control of your state of health. Notice the tremendous sense of satisfaction and emotional well-being you feel. And remember that the more positive feedback you give yourself, the faster and more effective your progress will be.

Achieving Mind-Body Harmony

The fourth Selective Awareness exercise, for mind-body harmony, will help you to get in touch with your breathing and with the flow of energy through your body.

Since you've already had experience with three different inductions for getting into the state of Selective Awareness, you've probably discovered the method, the collection of words and thoughts, that suits you best. Beginning with this exercise, you will go into Selective Awareness any way you prefer. If you are using a tape recorder, make your own tape, using your own words and images. Or you may be ready to dispense with the taped induction altogether and simply go into Selective Awareness by counting backward from ten to one, using whatever imagery works for you. In any case, the Mind-Body Harmony exercise begins after you have prepared yourself by getting into the state of Selective Awareness.

Relax, get comfortable, and read the exercise out loud once or twice. Now, using whatever method of induction you prefer, sit back, and allow yourself to experience Mind-Body Harmony.

If you are using a tape recorder, remember to shut it off whenever you want to allow yourself more time to experience a particular sensation. Let the act of switching the tape recorder off and on intensify your state of Selective Awareness, taking you even deeper into yourself.

Mind-Body Harmony Exercise

Use your own method for getting into the state of Selective Awareness. (If you are using a tape recorder, don't record the portions of the exercise in parentheses.)

When your "Yes" finger signals that you are deep in the state of Selective Awareness, tune in to a spot behind your eyes and between your ears. Let that spot be your center of mental energy and of peace of mind. When you have found that place of peace and energy, let your "Yes" finger lift.

Now tune in to the rhythm of your breathing. Realize that

breath means life and energy. Pick a spot at the center of your body as it relates to breathing (from the navel to the diaphragm — don't worry about where the center of the body *really* is, just feel the spot in relation to your breath). Let that spot represent physical energy. When you have reached it, let your "Yes" finger lift.

Now that you've found this mind-body harmony, let it flow through your body in rhythmic waves, allowing it to bathe your entire body from head to toe. Let the healing waves of mind-body energy flow over, under, around, and through your body, luxuriating in peace and joy until your "Yes" finger recognizes that this energy is working for you. And then allow the wave of energy to rise through your body into your mind, until you are filled with harmony, with joy and peace and love of life. And when you feel totally filled with this joyous mind-body harmony, allow your "Yes" finger to reaffirm that feeling of peace and joy.

When you are ready, count from one to five and return to the state of Social Awareness, happy to be alive, happy and at peace with your surroundings.

One — let yourself come up.

Two — feeling really good and relaxed.

Three — begin to open your eyes.

Four — wide awake now.

Five — refreshed, relaxed, comfortable, feeling good all over.

After you are thoroughly familiar with the sensation of mind-body harmony, you can use variations of this exercise to focus healing energy on any organ or part of the body you choose, simply by visualizing the area you want to work with, and directing the waves of energy to that area.

Remember to write down all the reactions of your body and mind as soon as you return to the state of Social Awareness. And don't forget to write down the flashes of insight that occur spontaneously at other times.

Body Assessment

The next Selective Awareness exercise is a body assessment, designed to let you get in touch with your body and how you feel about it right now, today.

When a part of the body gives negative feedback (through malfunction, pain, or unacceptable appearance), that part of the body may actually be "tuned out" — the self-system in effect refuses to acknowledge the existence of the affected area. The result is a misallocation of energy, bypassing the area where it is needed most. Through the Body Assessment exercise, you will learn to recognize the areas of your body where energy is blocked and what to do about those blocks. The information gained from the Body Assessment can also serve as a checklist for future exercises, to help you identify the areas that have been neglected in the process of energy absorption.

This exercise is a very short one on paper. Be sure to give yourself enough time to get thoroughly in touch with every part of your body.

Body Assessment Exercise

(Use your preferred method for getting into the state of Selective Awareness.)

As your "Yes" finger tells you you're in a comfortable state of Selective Awareness, that same signal will allow you to get in touch with information about yourself. Let that finger signal serve as a means of going deeper and deeper into yourself. As you go deeper and deeper, suddenly you come upon a mirror. See yourself reflected in that mirror. Imagine that you are looking into this mirror, seeing yourself reflected there, and that you accept your image with love and compassion. When it is all right to say, "How do you do, I like you and I accept you," allow your "Yes" finger to lift.

As you get acquainted with that image in the mirror, as you become more and more aware of yourself, see to what extent you can get in touch with all the parts of your body, becoming aware of them, but without actually reaching out and touching — just being in touch. Begin by getting in touch with your scalp and forehead and then wander over your forehead to your eyes. As you become increasingly aware of your scalp and forehead and eyes, note your feelings about those areas. (If you are receiving positive feedback from that area, let your "Yes" finger lift. If your "No" finger lifts, accept that information and go on with your assessment.) Now get in touch with your cheeks and mouth. Just getting in touch, feeling without reaching out, just becoming aware. Let that feeling of awareness extend over your shoulders to your chest.

And now open and close your eyes and as you do you will find that the feeling of being in touch with your body becomes even stronger. As soon as your eyes are closed pretend that you can't open them; you will find that your body is drifting into a very comfortable state of relaxation and acceptance. Allow yourself to assume that feeling of drifting. Allow yourself to become aware and to get in touch with your stomach, with the inside of your stomach. See what information you get. Any time you don't get any feeling of being in touch, then let your "No" finger signal.

Now let that awareness go into your hips; the sides of your hips, see to what extent you can become aware of the bones of your hip joint, and then let that awareness extend outward to the skin. Allow that feeling of getting in touch, of being aware, to extend to your thighs, the upper part of your legs. Now extend it downward to your calves and your ankles and feet. Imagine now that you're reaching out internally to become aware of your buttocks and your genitals. Just see what kind of information you can get from each part of your body, learning to understand what your body is telling you.

When your assessment of your body is complete, return to the state of Social Awareness, relaxed and comfortable, aware and accepting of your body.

(Count from one to five and return to the state of Social Awareness.)

As soon as you return to Social Awareness, review all the

information you have gained from your body assessment, and write down everything you have learned. Pay particular attention to the parts of your body with which you're out of touch or toward which you have negative feelings. This information will be a checklist for working with your body in the next exercise, the System Tune-up.

The more you tune out the parts of your body that don't give you good feedback — because of physical or emotional pain, or lack of acceptance — the more you deprive them of energy. When you spontaneously or subconsciously ignore a part of your body because you don't like the way it looks or feels, you aggravate the problem even more.

The key to any positive change is to become acceptable to yourself — not just as a body but as a person. Through Selective Awareness Therapy you can learn to accept yourself by breaking into the vicious cycle that is set up when you don't accept yourself with love and compassion. By getting in touch with your body and working to improve your self-image, you can learn to tune in and send energy to any part of your body you choose.

You May be Tuning Out Parts of Your Body

The case of Janice shows that this "tuning out" of areas of the body can be a serious matter. Janice came to me originally because she and her husband wanted very much to have a baby, but she had suffered a series of miscarriages. She stated that she was also frigid and nonorgasmic and that she had been suffering severe headaches since the age of seven.

Janice was cooperative and highly motivated, and in Selective Awareness she began to understand her own malfunctioning patterns. The habitual spontaneous abortions and current loss of sexual interest presented great marital difficulties, and since this was her third marriage it was important to her to clear up her problems.

Her personal history, as recorded in her notebook, centered mostly around sexual matters. She had her first sexual experience at the age of fifteen. At eighteen she became pregnant and had an abortion. A year later she became pregnant again, this time by a married man; this pregnancy too was aborted. The man divorced his wife, and he and Janice were married. This marriage lasted only two years, during which time she had a miscarriage.

Shortly after her divorce Janice married again. During the three years of her second marriage she had two more miscarriages. She stated that her sexual apathy was the cause of the breakup of this marriage. Now she and her third husband were eager to have children, but she continued to miscarry every time she got pregnant. Her most recent pregnancy had continued into the sixth month, when she was hospitalized after losing a great deal of blood. Obviously, her habitual spontaneous abortions were a health hazard, but she was unwilling to give up trying.

After reviewing her history, Janice set out to explore each incident in the state of Selective Awareness. As she oriented back to her first and second abortions, she experienced overwhelming guilt. Even though the man who got her pregnant the second time ultimately became her husband, she felt tremendously guilty about having broken up his home. Because of these feelings of guilt, her self-image was very poor. In her Selective Awareness body assessment, her uterus seemed to be saying, "You're not worthy of having a child. Pregnancy means abortion, whether it's induced or spontaneous."

Janice's assessment of her headache patterns also showed a sexual involvement. She oriented back to the age of seven, when her mother had caught her masturbating and had told her that if she continued her brain would shrivel up. Most of her subsequent headaches seemed to be related to masturbation and other forms of sexual activity. In view of her history, it seemed quite natural for Janice to tune out the sexual nature of her body. Her ideomotor finger signals revealed a healthy attitude toward her body except for the areas that are particularly female. Her responses were negative to her internal and external sexual organs and to her hips.

During one of her body assessment sessions, Janice saw herself meditating in the lotus position on a large cushion shaped like a uterus. To her surprise, she found herself orienting spontaneously back to birth. She discovered that she felt rejected by her parents and became aware that they had really wanted a boy. She reviewed her childhood and found that in trying to please her parents she had often wished that she could be a little boy.

In Selective Awareness image rehearsal, Janice was able to get rid of the resentment and anger that she felt toward her parents, as well as the anger and guilt she felt for herself. And she was able to send messages of acceptance, energy, and love to the areas of her body that she had tuned out, to her sexual organs and her hips. By her third Selective Awareness session, Janice had already noticed changes in herself that were also evident to other people, who began to comment on how well she was looking. She began to lose weight, and the fatty tissue she had carried on her hips all her life seemed to just melt away as she sent messages of love and acceptance to that area of her body.

About a year later, Janice and her husband and their new son paid me a visit. She had continued her therapy on her own, using image rehearsal to bring her pregnancy to a successful conclusion. Janice proudly announced that she had a Selective Awareness baby: No drugs, no anesthetic, no pain, all pleasure.

This case contains several interesting elements. From the time of birth, Janice had not wanted to be a woman. After her unfortunate early sexual experiences, she tuned out her womanhood to the point of losing her sexual drive. As she tuned out her sexuality she also tuned out her body and its physiological processes — her whole female structure was left helpless and without energy. The result was continual spontaneous abortions. At the same time, however, she wanted very much to reaffirm her womanhood by becoming a mother. As she tuned back in and sent messages of love and acceptance to all her organs, her interest in sex returned and she was able to carry her baby to term. She also found that her headaches cleared up spontaneously as a result of her body assessment work in Selective Awareness.

Preparing for a System Tune-Up

The System Tune-up exercise is designed to allow you to get further in touch with your internal organs and with your circulatory system. A great deal of the healing power of the body lies in the circulation of blood, which carries life-giving oxygen and nutrients to every cell and washes away impurities and dead matter.

As in the previous exercise, use your own method for getting into the state of Selective Awareness. As you read over the exercise, you will find more material in parentheses than in previous exercises. This is because each practice from now on will be more personal in nature. Only *you* know what symptom or area of the body you want to work with, and only you know what questions need to be asked and answered to put you in touch with the relevant symptom-producing events and other personal material. So read the exercise over carefully before you proceed.

After you have read the exercise, select a symptom, an organ, and/or an area of the body that needs attention. This is where you can use the information obtained from your Body Assessment. Now write down everything you can think of about the physical condition of that organ or area. Also record in your notebook your feelings about it, your emotional state at this time, and your feelings about the symptom you wish to address. After you have completed the System Tune-up exercise, you will find it interesting to compare your "before-and-after" notes.

System Tune-Up

(Use your own method for getting into the state of Selective Awareness.)

When your "Yes" finger signals that you are ready, take a deep breath and imagine that you are inhaling energy just as you are inhaling the oxygen that becomes part of your life cycle, part of life. Feel the relaxation that comes with this energy spreading throughout your body.

Imagine for a moment that you are a part of the air you breathe, entering into your lungs and relaxing the lung structures. As you breathe, let yourself become aware of your diaphragm, and the organs underneath the diaphragm — your stomach, and abdomen, and the muscles around your abdomen. Let them all go limp and loose. Now your breathing is rhythmic, comfortable. Let yourself drift deeper and deeper with every breath, and imagine that there is a halo of energy around your entire body.

As you work on yourself, try to become aware of the different organs inside your body, like your stomach and your heart and your liver. Imagine that each organ is involved in the healing process. Imagine your blood circulating into each organ, bringing in healing oxygen and nutrients and carrying away waste products. This is how healing takes place. Allow yourself also to become aware of nerves from each organ carrying information to your brain. And imagine the brain sending back healing impulses to the organs. (Visualize these organs, the circulation of blood, and healing messages in any way that makes sense to you.)

Now, as you count from ten to zero, focus on the particular part of your body about which you would like more information. (For headaches, for example, focus on the head and neck. If your stomach feels tight, spend some time becoming aware of the energy there. If you want to work on a weight problem, concentrate on the fatty tissue, so that you understand it as part of your body, accessible to energy exchange.)

Ten — let yourself drift deeper and deeper and allow yourself to get in touch with how that part of your body feels to you.

Nine — deeper and deeper, more and more aware.

Eight — all your muscles are limp and loose and relaxed.

Seven — completely and totally relaxed.

Six — more and more in touch with yourself and that part of your body you want to work with.

Five — drifting deeper and deeper. You may begin to question yourself with finger signals. Is it all right to relax and drift into a comfortable state of relaxation?

Four — drifting deeper and deeper.

Three, two, one, and zero.

Test the depth of your relaxation by pretending that you cannot open your eyes.

Now you may begin to influence your body and mind with the system of consider, consult, and consent. Ask yourself, "Is it all right to consider change?" Be aware of what your body tells you, of what your finger signals tell you. (If the answer is, "Yes, it's all right to consider change for the purpose of learning," ask the next question — for example, "Is it all right to get in touch with my head and neck and the feelings that may have produced the tension there?" As you question yourself, you may find that slashes of thought are entering your mind. Make room for them to come and go, and continue to question yourself. "Is it all right to begin to think in terms of change?" Allow the questions to be gentle and the change to be gradual. And realize that change is something that comes from within.)

As you work with yourself you may become aware of the emotion that accompanies your attention. Is there any anger toward the part of your body you're working with? Is there any hostility? Or fear? Or you may feel affection and gratitude. Notice what emotion you are dealing with at this particular time.

Now ask yourself again if it would be all right to consider change for healing, for health. When your "Yes" finger signals consent, then visualize your body and see that organ or structure functioning ideally, as you would like it to. Breathe deeply, and allow your breath and blood to purify the area you are working with, washing it with oxygen and nutrients, carrying away waste products and impurities.

When you have a good, clear picture of yourself functioning as you would like to function, mind and body working together in harmony to heal the affected area of your body, suggest to your "Yes" finger that it will move, so that this visual picture or image of yourself as you would like to be will be just as clear tomorrow and the day after as it is today.

Now, whenever you are ready, allow yourself to realize that the comfort and well-being that you feel are going to stay with you as you return to a state of Social Awareness. As you count up from one to five, hold the sensation of relaxed alertness and well-being in your mind.

One — let yourself come up.

Two — feeling relaxed and good.

Three — whenever you're ready, open your eyes.

Four — wide awake.

Five — relaxed, refreshed, and feeling alert.

Now that you have finished the System Tune-up exercise, take the time to review your experience in writing, with particular attention to the organ, area of your body, or symptom you have been working with. Then go back and re-read the notes you made before doing this practice.

When you are thoroughly familiar with this exercise, you can adapt it to practically any situation where you want to give a specific problem area a boost toward health. Selective Awareness Therapy is, above all, a personal and flexible system.

Six

Learning to Deal with Headaches, Muscle Spasm, and Other Pains

All pain is a warning signal of a disturbance in the smooth functioning of the body, and no pain should ever be ignored. However, as we have seen, when a muscle or organ is sensitized in the presence of a strong negative emotion, it may continue to react with pain whenever that emotion occurs again in the future. Many of the aches and pains that we live with fall into this category — including most headaches and muscular pains like leg cramps or muscle spasms in the neck and back.

The next Selective Awareness exercise deals with this type of pain. Before you begin, pinpoint the symptom and area of your body that you want to work with, and write down your thoughts and feelings about that area and symptom.

This exercise is only a guideline. As you read it over, or as you make your tape, adapt it to your personal needs, inserting your own words wherever they're appropriate. If you're working on a muscle spasm in the back of your neck, for example, instead of saying, "Now go to the part of your body that you want to work with and let all those muscles relax," you might say, "Now allow your attention to focus on the back of your neck, and let all of the muscles there relax." Read the exercise with extra care, noting where you will want to tailor it to meet your own particular needs.

The emotional component in cases of muscle pain and spasm of long duration is frequently overwhelming anger. This was true of Natalie, for example, whose neck and back pain were constantly restimulated by her emotional state. In these cases, the biochemical response of the parasympathetic nervous system influences the autonomic nervous system, producing a muscle spasm.

Remember that muscles that have been sensitized in the presence of emotion are particularly vulnerable to pain and spasm. The corollary is that when the tension that has been causing the pain is relieved, the prevailing emotion is likely to be released as well. This means that when you're working with pain in the state of Selective Awareness, you're likely to find a lot of emotional material and long-buried memories coming up at the same time.

Obviously, this material can't be predicted or your response to it anticipated. When you do get in touch with the emotional content of a symptom, if you feel like looking for the symptom- producing event, give yourself the time necessary — turn off the tape recorder if you are using one — allowing that action to deepen your state of Selective Awareness. Then consult with yourself — "Would it be OK to investigate this emotion, to find out what's behind it?" When your "Yes" finger signals consent, relax and consider your next question to yourself. Your mind will guide you, with an image, or a memory of an event, or with the next question to be asked. If nothing comes into your mind, just relax for a few minutes, and then ask if it's time to go on. Just remember that there's no pressure on you to perform in any particular way, and if you use the system of consider, consult, and consent and pay attention to the information given to you by your ideomotor finger signals, you are completely in control of the material your mind presents.

The following exercise is designed to increase the flow of energy and the circulation of blood to wherever you direct it. And for pain relief, oxygen is better than aspirin, emotional content or no!

Dealing with Pain

Remember it is easier to change a pain into a more acceptable feeling, such as warmth, than it is to stop it. It is easier to let go gradually than to arbitrarily set up time limits.

(Use you own method for getting into the state of Selective Awareness.)

Now go back to that space behind your eyes and between your ears, that point of mental energy and peace of mind. Go back to your own private space, a space where you can be by yourself and for yourself. Imagine what it feels like to allow your brain wave activity to slow down to a nice, rhythmic pattern, discharging all the tension and static that have collected there. Just drift into the rhythm of peace, and let yourself realize that you are in a powerful space, a very powerful space for controlling the functions of your body.

Now imagine that messages of peace are radiating out from that point of mental energy, going out to all your muscles, allowing them to let go and discharge their tension. Now go to the part of your body that you want to work with and let all those muscles relax. Imagine that you can feel all the individual muscles releasing their tension, radiating it away to be replaced by the free flow of healthy energy.

Now ask yourself for your consent, the consent of the inner mind, to let go of the pain. When your "Yes" finger signals consent to healing, consent to letting go of the pain, you will find that you are in touch with the part of your body that you want to work with.

Imagine that you can feel the nerve impulses from your brain to your muscles in that part of your body, and allow those nerve impulses to break up the pain and spasm. Literally feel muscles releasing the tension that causes pain, feel the pain float away, to be replaced by the comfortable warmth of the life-giving circulation of blood and energy. As your muscles let go and relax, send them a message of warmth and reassurance. "You're part of me. I love you! I love you!"

Imagine that all the excess negative energy in your body

is being discharged and translated into positive energy that can be available for healing. Imagine that you can actually see healing taking place as blood rushes into the area, cleansing and purifying it of all tension, breaking up pain and spasm, washing the area clean.

As you feel that positive energy moving in your body, allow your "Yes" finger to affirm and strengthen that sensation.

Now, as you count backward from ten to zero, imagine that you are beginning to float, to drift even deeper inside yourself so that you can see the whole connection of mind and body. See how your mind can send messages to your body, subconscious messages of relaxation and healing.

Ten — drifting deeper and deeper.

Nine — all your muscles limp and loose.

Eight — tune in to the flow of energy in your body, and the rhythm of your breathing.

Seven — let that flow of energy involve all the muscles in your entire body.

Six, five — feel that energy flow, particularly in those muscles that need to let go and relax.

Four — as you begin to feel even more comfortable and more relaxed, any lingering discomfort is washed away.

Three, two — completely and totally relaxed.

One, and zero.

Now see yourself as you would like to feel, free of pain and the necessity of pain. And remember that the process of healing is going to continue, that your mind and body will continue in the harmony of healing after you've completed this exercise.

Now, as you count from one to five, notice how very relaxed and comfortable you feel.

(Count from one to five and return to the state of Social Awareness, using any words or images that are effective for you.)

As soon as the headaches, muscle spasms, or other pains begin to respond to the attention you are giving yourself in Selective Awareness, give yourself some positive feedback. This exercise will be similar to the last one, but it will incorporate all the positive changes that you're experiencing. Congratulate yourself on the progress you're making, and don't forget to thank yourself for letting those beneficial changes take place.

How Anger Can Interfere with Healing

Skip's case history is interesting because it clearly shows how an obvious physical injury, with the physical symptoms of pain and spasm, is tied up with a thought-emotion process that interferes with proper healing.

Skip had been an Olympic weight lifter, but in the past three years he had injured his back three times while lifting weights. His health inventory showed that the last injury was the most severe, incurred when he attempted to lift, from a squatting position, a weight 80 pounds heavier than he had ever lifted before. This injury resulted in sudden, excruciating back pain that flared up periodically, finally shifting to his lower back and buttocks, with radiating pain down his legs into his hamstrings.

X-rays of the affected area showed no bone injury, and Skip's doctor informed him that his pain was due to severe muscle spasms. But despite physical therapy, massage, and muscle relaxants, the pain did not decrease. After making a tape recording for himself to work with his muscle spasms, Skip experienced some relief from the pain, and by the third session he rated himself as "75 percent improved."

In exploring his condition in the state of Selective Awareness, Skip found that his backaches were a reflection of his retirement from Olympic weight-lifting activities and that his injury served as an excuse for no longer participating fully in the sport. How could he possibly be in the Olympics with a bad back? He also became aware of a great deal of anger directed at himself for inappropriately lifting such a great weight.

Once Skip understood that his lingering backache was an excuse for no longer participating in the Olympics and that his anger was interfering with the proper dynamics of healing, he retrained his body to follow the natural sequence of healing and improved rapidly.

Seven

Learning to Influence Your Circulatory System

If you suspect that your blood pressure is high, do see your doctor and follow his or her advice. The exercises presented in this section can be used in connection with medication until that medication is no longer needed, but nothing can replace a thorough medical checkup.

Before you begin to work with your blood pressure, it's helpful to know a little about your heart and circulatory system, and about the mechanics of hypertension (high blood pressure).

The Heart and Circulatory System

The importance of blood to the life process is obvious. Blood bathes every cell in the body continuously, bringing oxygen and nutrients and carrying away waste products. The blood circulates constantly through the body, entering the heart through the right auricle. From the right auricle, the blood passes through a valve into the right ventricle, and the contraction of that ventricle sends the blood into the lungs where the red blood cells pick up oxygen. From there the oxygenated blood is returned to the heart through the left auricle and is then pumped through the mitral valve into the left ventricle. The left ventricle is the major pump from which all arterial blood, loaded with oxygen, is pumped into all parts of the body. This oxygenated blood leaves the left ventricle through

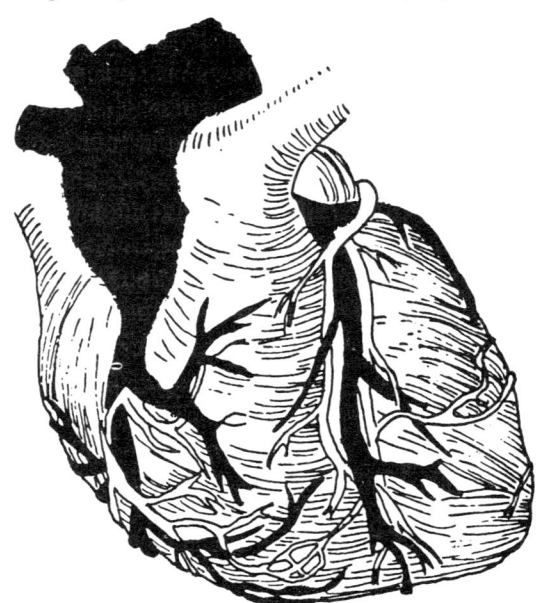

Heart and Coronary Vessels

the aorta, which separates into many smaller arteries much like the branches of a tree. This branching continues throughout the body until the blood reaches the cellular level by way of minute arterioles, or capillaries.

At this point, oxygen and nutrients are exchanged and waste products are picked up by the blood. Blood is returned to the heart through the venules and veins. In the course of this circulation, every part of the body is supplied with arterial blood bringing oxygen and nutrients to the cells, and waste products are picked up and blood returned to the heart by way of the venous system.

While arterial blood is actively pumped through the body by the action of the heart, blood returning to the heart by way of venous circulation has no such pump available. The return of venous blood occurs through the pumping action of muscle contraction, squeezing blood through the veins through one-way valves which allow blood flow only in the direction of the heart.

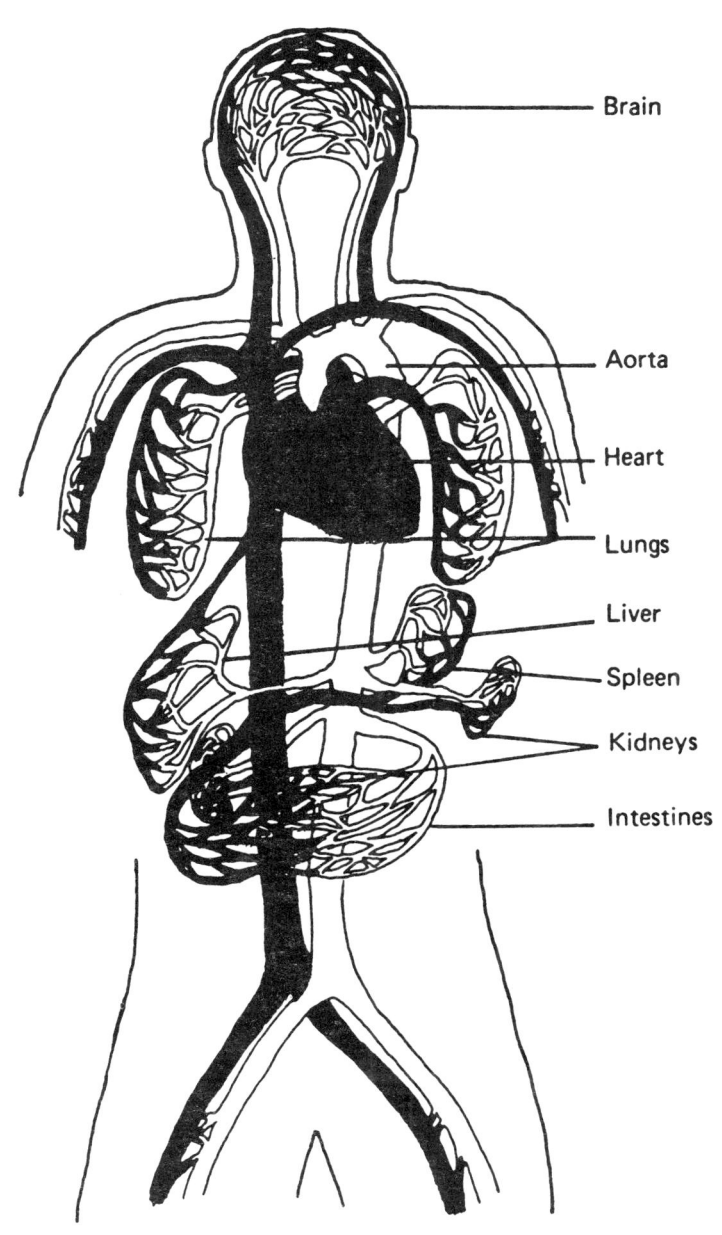

Brain

Aorta

Heart

Lungs

Liver

Spleen

Kidneys

Intestines

Circulatory System

The walls of the arteries themselves are surrounded by circular muscles. These walls are elastic and give way with each heart beat, allowing continuous and consistent pressure within the arteries. When the heart beats harder than usual, as in physical stress or in the emotional states of fear, anger, and tension, the blood pressure may rise as the heart contracts and then fall back to normal when the heart expands again. But when the muscles of the arterial system are in a relative state of spasm, the arteries are not flexible enough to expand with the flow of blood, and the blood pressure remains high.

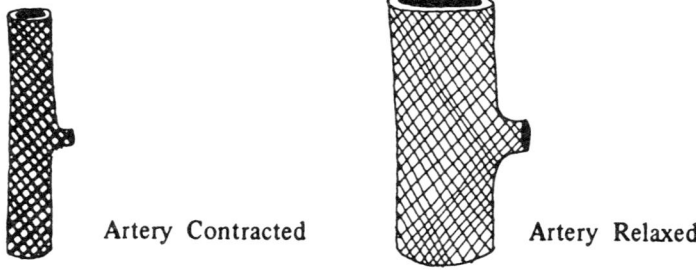

Artery Contracted   Artery Relaxed

Hypertension

Essential hypertension — high blood pressure without an obvious physical cause — is the leading cause of death in the United States. Numerous clinical investigations have revealed that the onset of essential hypertension is related to the effects of stress and negative emotions — particularly to the effects of anxiety, frustration, and anger, which, as we have seen, induce the sympathetic nervous system to release chemicals that affect the autonomic nervous system. This biochemical response to negative emotion has the direct effect of constricting the arterial components of the circulatory system, so that all the arteries go into spasm, including those of the skeletal muscles and internal organs. This contraction of the arteries and arterioles is responsible for the elevation of the blood pressure.

Another result of this constriction is a decreased blood supply to the internal organs, a condition called *ischemia*. Since the blood vessels in the kidneys are very reactive to emotional and physical stimuli, the kidneys produce a chemical called *renotensin*, which further raises the blood pressure. Insufficient blood supply to the kidneys alone is capable of causing the kidneys to produce enough renotensin to raise the overall blood pressure.

In working with hypertension through Selective Awareness, you will learn to follow your blood vessels from their origin in the heart through every part of your body, helping them to be relaxed, pliable, and physiologically normal. Study the drawings of the heart and circulatory system, and do the exercise twice a day at first, until you're as familiar with your heart and arteries as you are with the freeway you drive on the way to work. Soon you will be able to feel your arteries as the blood pulses through them, and you will be able to relax them when they are in spasm, just as you would relax your hand if it were clenched into a fist.

Anginal Pain

As we have seen, the arteries are surrounded by cross-bands of smooth muscles that are capable of contracting until they are completely closed. When this localized spasm affects the coronary arteries, the result is ischemia of the heart muscle, which may be felt as anginal pain. This is particularly likely to occur at times of emotional stress or physical exertion. The Selective Awareness exercise for hypertension can easily be adapted for working with anginal pain. As you follow your blood vessels from their origin in the heart, pay particular attention to the coronary arteries, the first branching of the major blood vessels. Practice seeing those arteries relax, allowing an abundant supply of fresh, oxygenated blood to bathe the heart muscle. See those arteries clear and pliable and free of spasm.

Image rehearsal is particularly helpful in relieving anginal pain. In the long run, it's more helpful than nitroglycerin.

Before you do the following exercise, take a few minutes to write down everything you know about your blood pressure, including anything your doctor has told you. Note also your emotional state right now, especially any feelings you might have about your heart and arteries. And if you have any idea about the emotional component of your hypertension or anginal pain, good — write it down. This information can be very useful in later image rehearsal.

Helping Your Circulatory System

(Use the method you prefer for getting into the state of Selective Awareness.)

When your "Yes" finger signals that you are deep into the state of Selective Awareness, let yourself become totally aware of your breath. Tune in to the rhythm of your breathing and let it work for you. Let your breath flow through your body in a rhythm of relaxation. Notice how comfortable and relaxed you feel, and let that feeling of relaxation become intensified with every breath. As you breathe you can let that rhythm become a source of energy. As you inhale, let the oxygen that flows into your lungs carry energy to every part of your body. And as you exhale, release from your body all negative energy and negative emotions along with any waste products, like carbon dioxide. Let the rhythm of breathing flow like a wave through your body, carrying energy to where it is needed most.

As you drift deeper and deeper, let yourself return to that familiar place in your mind, the spot of mental energy and harmony. Allow that feeling of peace and energy to flow through your body, carried by the rhythm of your breath.

Now, when your "Yes" finger signals that you are ready, you will begin an imaginary trip through all your arteries, checking to make sure that they are clean and pliable every-where in your body, because as your mind produces the image of perfection, your body will follow suit. Your body will be busy absorbing deposits in the arteries to make them clean and keep them pliable and flexible. Imagine that you can look inside your heart and see all the valves working exactly as they are supposed to. Follow the major aorta and its branches upward into your neck, and head, and see that wherever they branch they are pliable and clean. Imagine how the extensions of those arteries will supply your brain with energy in the form of oxygen and nutrients.

Now follow those blood vessels downward, realizing that every part of you, every bone, every muscle, and every organ, including your skin, is supplied by a branching network of blood vessels. And every one of the arteries and arterioles in that network is relaxed, pliable, and capable of giving way to each heartbeat so that the blood rushes into a cushioned cavity. Let yourself realize that it is this elasticity of your blood vessels that allows your blood pressure to be low. Remember that your blood pressure is capable of being low and that your arteries are capable of relaxing, just like your muscles.

Now think for a moment in terms of permanent relaxation, permanent elasticity. See your arteries clear, pliant, flexible, and remember that your blood pressure is capable of remaining low. Imagine that there is no need for the blood pressure to rise because when your body and mind work together in harmony, they can handle any situation that comes up, without the need for your blood pressure to rise. Just as your muscles have learned to relax, your arteries can too.

Follow those arteries now through your abdomen into the kidneys, and remember that there is no need for your kidneys to produce anything that would lead to hypertension. Imagine your kidneys saying, "No need to raise that pressure." Feel the flow of blood through the kidneys, supplying them with oxygen and nutrients, everything they need to do their job.

Now feel the blood flow into your pelvis, see your arteries branching, supplying your intestines, branching and supplying your legs. Feel the blood vessels going all the way down in your legs until they reach the tip of every toe.

Remember that your arteries can be permanently clean, pliable, flexible. Your arteries can learn to remain relaxed so that your blood pressure can remain normal. Remember that you have the power to regulate the functions of your own body, and let that knowledge expand into a feeling of comfort and well- being in your body. Let the knowledge that you have control over your body give you a tremendous sense of comfort and security.

Let yourself drift deeper and deeper into your body and tune in to your pulse as a reflection of your heartbeat. Tune in to your pulse — hear it and feel it in your body. Take a moment to concentrate on your pulse, to enjoy the strong rhythm of your heart pumping blood to every part of your body.

As you feel the pulse of your blood carrying oxygen and energy through your arteries to every part of your body, allow yourself to drift even deeper, feeling even more comfortable and relaxed. Remember that deeper means internalizing your awareness so that you can become aware of different feelings and functions within your body. Deeper means becoming more influential in altering your bodily functions toward health.

Now, as you continue to tune in to your body, once again follow the flow of blood through the kidneys. Imagine your kidneys doing their job, filtering out the waste products, becoming an even more effective filter, breaking up and discharging waste products from your body. Let that sensation of knowing that your kidneys are performing their task give you a tremendous sense of confidence in your power to regulate your body functions, so that when you count from one to five you will return to a state of Social Awareness feeling comfortable, confident, and very, very relaxed.

(Count from one to five, using whatever words and images you prefer, and return to the state of Social Awareness.)

Give Yourself Credit

As soon as you notice positive changes from working with your blood pressure in Selective Awareness, give yourself some positive feedback. This exercise will be similar to the last one, but as you take your imaginary trip through your circulatory system, compliment yourself on the work you've already done. Notice how clean and pliable your arteries are, and allow yourself to recognize that your efforts have already resulted in positive change; this positive feedback will also reinforce the idea of permanent change in the direction of health. Every time you reflect back to your system the advances that have already been made, you clear the way for even further progress.

As mentioned earlier, negative emotional states contribute greatly to hypertension and to anginal pain. Although the image rehearsal of the previous exercise can be dramatically effective in lowering blood pressure or relieving angina all by itself, you may want to explore the emotional causes as well. If you decide to do this, once you are in the state of Selective Awareness, use the system of consider, consult, and consent to explore the emotional basis for your hypertension or angina. Would it be all right to look into that subject? Would it be all right to get in touch with the emotional state that leads to high blood pressure? When your "Yes" finger signals affirmation, allow your mind to return to a time when your blood pressure was elevated, or when you experienced anginal pain. Take a good look at the scene. Where are you? What are you doing? Who else is there? And what are you feeling? Don't relive the experience, just review it. Let your mind review three or four of the symptom-producing events, noting especially the emotional thread common to all of them. Remember to use the system of consider, consult, and consent, and to respect the information given to you by your ideomotor finger signals.

Now go back over those same symptom-producing events, using image rehearsal to see the situation exactly as it was — except that you are calm, and your body has no need to respond to your emotional state by elevating your blood pressure. See yourself functioning smoothly, as you would like to function, in a situation that would previously have been upsetting.

When you return to the state of Social Awareness, review and write down everything you have learned about the relationship between your emotional state and your blood pressure or anginal pain. You can use this information to control your response to emotionally stressful or anxiety-provoking situations in the future.

Eight

Weight Reduction

The following report appeared in *U.S. Medicine*, February 1, 1968.

Group hypnotherapy reportedly resulted in substantial weight loss and improvements in personal appearance among a group of overweight women, many of whom were classified as "recalcitrant obese patients."

Peter H. C. Mutke, M.D., said the patients were treated for about an hour each week over a period of ten weeks. They were separated into four groups.

Treatment included hypnotherapy, hypnoanalysis, and "image rehearsal," and about 85 percent of the patients learned the use of autohypnosis.

At the end of the program, the mean weight loss for the group was 15.6 pounds, or 8 percent of the mean body weight.

The patients registered weight loss ranging from 0 to 32 pounds. In addition, all patients experienced a tremendous feeling of well being, an increased interest in relating to others, and showed a striking improvement in personal appearance.

They considered themselves sufficiently worthwhile to make the effort to dress well and improve grooming. Their awareness for semantics and their change in philosophy brought frequent dramatic improvements in their marriages.

"Image rehearsal" was the most important therapeutic procedure to achieve a desensitization of unfavorable stimuli, to learn new attitudes, discipline, and orientations.

It was this experience, working with group hypnotherapy and hypnoanalysis in overweight patients in 1968, that led to the formulation of a system for weight loss using Selective Awareness Therapy.

Good health begins with good nutrition. Food is basic to vitality and health. Food is also an emotionally charged subject, particularly for people who are overweight. When eating habits get tied up with boredom, depression, loneliness, anger, or feelings of worthlessness, the regulatory mechanisms of the body that deal with the absorption of food are thrown out of balance, and so is the mechanism that's supposed to signal, "That's enough, stop eating now."

Of course, sensible eating and exercise are important, not only in weight loss but in maintaining health, vitality, and energy. But most diets fail, and they fail because the emotional component is not recognized or dealt with. Through Selective Awareness Therapy, you can learn to work with the emotions that contribute to overweight, to change your body image, and to retrain the regulatory mechanisms and absorption process of your body.

There is almost always an emotional component in weight problems, whether you're overweight or thin as a rail. You may know someone who seems to eat twice as much as you do and yet never gains an ounce. Of course, how much you eat and what you eat are important, but equally important is the way your body makes use of food. In Selective Awareness Therapy, it doesn't matter what you weigh or how many pounds you want to lose. What does matter in losing weight is getting in touch with your body — with those deposits of fatty tissue and with your feelings about yourself and food — so that you can retrain its absorption process.

Through Selective Awareness Therapy you will learn to evaluate and reprogram your eating habits and help your body to learn new patterns of intestinal absorption of food and reabsorption of stored fat.

Don't Be a Fat Rat

In evaluating your eating habits, please note that where and how you eat can be as important as what you eat. University research on rats reveals some interesting facts about the importance of eating habits. In one experiment, two groups of rats were used, an experimental group and a control group. The control group was fed a diet of normal caloric content. These rats were fed every day at the same time, in a quiet atmosphere, and they maintained their weight very nicely. The rats in the experimental group, however, were fed the same food, in the same amounts, but at irregular intervals, sometimes at 10 in the morning, sometimes at 5 in the afternoon, but only once a day. And one more element was added — these rats were fed on a conveyor belt, a belt that moved the food from one end of the cage to the other. Rats are fast learners, and it took most of them only one trip to learn that if they hadn't finished their food before it moved from "here" to "there," the food would be gone. So they learned to gulp their meals down on the move — copying the behavior of many people who are overweight. And these meal-skipping, food-gulping rats gained weight, even though they ate no more than their brothers and sisters in the control group.

Experimental rats don't have a choice about where and when they take their meals — but you do.

Many people who are concerned about their weight tend to skip meals, believing that if they eat less, they will weigh less. But what actually happens when you eat at irregular intervals is that your body literally doesn't know when it's going to be fed again. The irregularity sets off an internal reaction in your metabolic system of absorbing every calorie you take in, whether it's needed for energy or not. And if those calories aren't burned up as fuel for energy, they get stored as fatty tissue.

There is an internal mechanism that establishes a balance in the body to let us know we should stop eating — because we've had enough food. This mechanism is disrupted when we eat irregularly or skip meals and also when we eat so quickly that the body doesn't have time to signal, "that's enough."

This mechanism is similar to the mechanism in your automobile that regulates the flow of gasoline to the engine. Without that control, the car would run for a while, sputter, stop, run and sputter again. It would not be at all an efficient engine.

Animals have a similar regulatory mechanism; you rarely see a fat animal in the wild, even where there is an abundance of food. It is when animals become domesticated and pick up human habits that they become fat. The lesson for us is clear — if we give our bodies a chance to return to a state of balance, they will tell us what and how much we should eat.

You Won't Need a Diet

One thing you don't need to worry about in Selective Awareness Therapy is going on a diet. You've probably already been on at least one diet, and you know how difficult it is to give up all your favorite foods, to begrudge every bit you put in your mouth, to try to subsist on grapefruit and skim milk. That kind of dieting inevitably leads to frustration, a relapse into old eating habits, guilt, and regaining all the weight you've lost — because your body hasn't been retrained, but only forced into an impossibly rigid mold. If your body and mind aren't working together in harmony, it's next to impossible to lose weight and keep it off.

Most people who are concerned about their weight have some idea of what good nutrition really is. To lose weight with Selective Awareness Therapy or any other plan, you do have to learn to eat sensibly. So get yourself a book on nutrition, and read up on what your body needs to maintain life and health. (I recommend *Let's Eat Right to Keep Fit* by Adelle Davis.) The study of food can be fascinating in itself. Just don't think of it as "going on a diet," with calories to be counted and portions to be measured. The most important thing in taking weight off and keeping it off is your self — your self-image, self-evaluation, self-appreciation, and self-understanding.

At the beginning of your weight reduction program you need to exercise a certain amount of discretion and to investigate alternate choices for some of your favorite foods. For example, you may find that learning to enjoy skim milk rather than whole milk can save you many calories a day. By learning about the simple substitutions of low-calorie foods for high-calorie ones, you can enjoy the same meals that your family eats and still lose weight. Once you've achieved your ideal weight, you will probably find that it doesn't matter what you eat, because the goal of Selective Awareness Therapy is body-mind harmony. In weight reduction, that means re-establishing the self-regulating mechanism that allows your body to use what it needs for fuel and to pass the rest through without adding pounds and inches.

When you decide to lose weight through Selective Awareness Therapy, there's a simple thing you can do right away — stop weighing yourself every day. That mechanical conscience, the bathroom scale, is a depressing and destructive device for the person who wants to lose weight. If you've gained half a pound, you're depressed. And even if you've lost weight, you can't possibly reach your goal in only one day. So put your scale in the back of the closet, and if you *must* have that external verification of how you're doing, get it out and weigh yourself once a week. Once a month would be even better. It took a long time for your body to put on that extra weight, and it's not going to disappear overnight.

Learning Healthy Eating Patterns

There are several things you can do to help your body return to healthy eating patterns. The first, as we've seen, is to eat at regular times, so that your body knows when its next meal is coming.

The second important factor is exercise. Every pound of excess weight in your body represents 3,500 calories above your body's fuel requirement. Most adults require between 1,200 and 3,000 calories, depending on their level of physical activity. Even a couple of five-minute sessions of mild calisthenics every day can be useful in restoring muscle tone, as well as using up calories. An ideal exercise, one that stimulates and tones your whole body, is jogging, alternating with brisk walking. Start slowly — even a couple of laps around the local high school track at first can help you to get back in touch with the way your body is supposed to function. Bicycling is another excellent form of exercise. Don't be afraid to work up a sweat. And if your body is sore the first couple of days, don't worry about it — that's a sign you're doing good work. Your muscles may be astounded, even outraged, at first, but they'll love you for it later.

The third point to consider is that food is important, emotionally as well as physically; mealtimes should be fun, a bright spot in the day, something to look forward to. Emotional upset at mealtime can confuse the regulatory mechanisms just like skipping meals or eating at irregular hours. We'll go into this in more depth in just a moment.

And fourth, it's important to get an *overview* of your eating habits, as well as a *review* of what you've eaten. A good time to get such an overview is at the grocery store. If you buy only food that you know you can eat, you won't be tempted by having goodies around the house to nibble on.

The most important tool in getting an overview of your eating patterns is your "food diary." With it you can help yourself to answer some intriguing questions. Why does your body store fat inappropriately? Do you overeat when you're angry, or when you're sad, or when you're bored? Does food compensate for something else that's lacking? Is food a consolation to you? Selective Awareness Therapy will help you to get at the emotional basis for your own personal reaction to food.

The first step in getting at this emotional basis for overeating is to assess your eating habits. You can do this by keeping a food diary for one week. Don't try to change your eating habits or to count calories; just write down, for one week, everything you eat. Your diary should show not only what you eat but also when and where. Do you eat standing up at the refrigerator? Or sitting in front of the television? Every time you eat something, note your emotional state. How are you feeling in general? How do you feel about yourself? And how do you feel about the food as you eat it?

The patterns that emerge in only a week will be very revealing. For one thing, you may find that you are drawn to a particular kind of food — sweets, perhaps, or bread and pastries. It's easy to develop a physical dependence, even an addiction, to some kinds of foods, especially those high in sugar or carbohydrates. Or you may actually be deficient in some nutrients, no matter how well-balanced your diet, simply because your body doesn't make proper use of the food you take in. Keeping a food diary for a week will let you see all kinds of patterns, both physical and emotional, that you may not have noticed before.

Another thing that frequently shows up in the food diaries of overweight people is that mealtimes are or were at one time punitive events. Identifying anger or guilt with eating can quickly lead to disruption of the absorption mechanism, causing storage of excess fat. So one of the goals in the Selective Awareness Therapy program is to make mealtimes fun.

Your food diary should tell you specifically: How often do I eat? How much do I eat? When do I eat? And, most importantly, how do I eat? In the car going to work? On the conveyor belt? Enjoying your food is critical to reversing the imbalance in your metabolic system.

The Emotions that Make You Overeat

One of the more important factors in weight loss is the self-evaluation of obesity dynamics. In this area, no two people are alike. We all respond uniquely to life situations, and that goes for eating habits and obesity dynamics as well as everything else. There are, however, certain emotional patterns that are common among overweight people. For one thing, food is frequently used for consolation. If that's your pattern, it will show up in your food diary. When you've got your hand in the cookie jar and your head says, "Get your hand out of there," does your hand come out empty or full? And how do you feel at those times? When you get in touch with those feelings, you will know whether you eat because you're angry, or sad, or bored, or dissatisfied with your life.

An important point to note in your daily log is how you feel when you eat beyond your conscious discretion, when your mind says "No" and your mouth chews and swallows anyway.

Another important thing that needs to be evaluated is the quality of your diet. By the time much of our food has been homogenized, purified, neutralized, and restored, much of its nutritional value has been destroyed. In the long run, the quality of the fuel you take in determines that of the energy you put out.

How did your body's absorption mechanism get off on the wrong track? When and why did your obesity dynamic develop? You probably already have a pretty good idea of when you overeat — "When I'm depressed food cheers me up," or "I get so mad at myself for eating three cookies, I figure it doesn't matter, and I end up eating the whole package." When you say, "No, I don't want to eat that" but something makes you go ahead and eat it anyway, you know that that something is very powerful. It has taught your emotions and your body to work together in a way that is destructive to their proper biological functioning.

Getting Your Absorption Mechanism Back on Track

Through Selective Awareness Therapy you can evaluate both your body and your emotions to see what has stimulated the accumulation of excess weight. Most overweight people are out of touch with their bodies, cut off from contact. They turn away from the unpleasant visual and conceptual feedback they receive. But when you tune out and turn away, you rob yourself of your only means of directing energy and attention to the areas that need the most help.

One technique you will learn in this chapter is to have a dialogue with yourself in front of the mirror, talking to every part of yourself. When you make an effort to talk to yourself, you learn a lot. You may find your body telling you, "You are neglecting me," or "Help me," or "Poor me," or "Fat is safe, it keeps people away." Acknowledge yourself. You only have one body and you may as well accept it; nobody's going to give you another one. By accepting your body, you can stop this vicious cycle of tuning out and gaining weight. When you tune out, your body gets the message that it's just a storage place for fat.

Because the whole area of food and eating habits is so important, three Selective Awareness exercises are included in this section. The first is a review exercise, to help you get in touch with your body and emotions; the second is a body assessment exercise; and the third stresses image rehearsal and confidence building.

Getting in Touch with Your Eating Patterns

In the next Selective Awareness exercise, you will pick a day in the recent past, a good day when you ate sensibly, when things were going well and you felt good about yourself. You will spend some time getting in touch with your positive feelings on that day, enhancing them and making them your own. Then you will orient back to a day when things weren't going so well, when you ate unwisely and didn't enjoy it, to see what you can learn from that experience. You will then be able to pinpoint and understand the link between your emotions and your eating patterns. Be sure to record this information in your notebook.

This exercise is a short one on paper, but if you make a

tape, give yourself plenty of time to explore your new awareness, to really get in touch with what you are feeling.

Getting in Touch with Your Eating Patterns — Practice

(Use whatever method you prefer for getting into the state of Selective Awareness.)

When your "Yes" finger signals that you are relaxed and comfortable in the state of Selective Awareness, allow your mind to let go of any remaining tension or mental activity, as you slip into an even deeper state of tranquility. Take a deep breath and as you let it out release any areas of tension in your body. Pay particular attention to your neck and shoulders. Let them relax, feel the weight lifting off your shoulders, the weight of daily activities, all the burdens you carry, let them go and feel them fall away. Enjoy the pleasure of breathing as you take in air, energy; enjoy exhaling, imagining how good it feels to exhale tension and waste products. See yourself inhaling energy and exhaling tension until you feel that your body is covered with a soothing comforter of relaxation.

Now let an image of yourself enter your mind, a picture of yourself as you would like to look, as you're going to look. Picture yourself as you would like to feel, as you are going to feel. When that image of yourself is firm in your mind, let your "Yes" finger signal affirmation.

Now let your mind go back to a particularly good day, a recent day that you enjoyed, a day when food was not especially important to you, but when you ate properly and enjoyed yourself. Review that day from morning to night, and notice the pleasure you feel, the sense of accomplishment, the general sense of well- being in saying, "That was a good day. When all days are like that I know that losing weight will become an automatic process." And remember that what you can do for one day you can do for two days, or ten; taking pleasure in eating healthfully can become a general attitude that will last for life.

Now review a day when things did not go so well, when you ate more than you wanted to eat, when you disregarded your better judgment and went on a binge. Give yourself love and compassion as you review that day, from morning to night.

When you are ready, ask yourself, would it be all right to find out about my emotional state on that day? When your "Yes" finger signals affirmation, ask yourself, "How did I feel on that day? Why did I eat that way?"

Now just relax and watch the thoughts and feelings that come into your mind. See yourself eating something on that particular day and notice how you feel. What is your emotional state? Give yourself compassion, understanding, and the desire to learn, as you identify the emotion you felt on that day. And as you identify that emotion, let your "No" finger lift. Stay with that feeling and welcome it, because you are going to learn something very valuable from it — something that will help you to change your eating patterns.

Now count backward from ten to one, and as you do so, allow yourself to view your emotional state with compassion, with understanding, and with a desire to learn.

(Count back from ten to one, using whatever words and images are appropriate for you.)

Once again, review that particular day when your eating pattern or habits got the better of your desire to take proper care of your body. When your "No" finger lifts you will find that the link between your emotions and your eating habits is becoming very clear. Let that awareness and knowledge stay with you, in a comfortable and compassionate way, as you count from one to five and return to a state of Social Awareness.

(Count from one to five, using your own words and images, and return to the state of Social Awareness feeling relaxed, comfortable, and very alert.)

Now that you've done the first Selective Awareness exercise for weight reduction, you may want to try a few sessions using only your favorite induction, so that you can explore more thoroughly the emotions and information you have begun to uncover. You may also orient back to earlier symptom-producing events to get at the basis of your weight problem. Just remember to use the system of consider, consult, and consent, and to pay attention to your ideomotor finger signals. Some people find that their most valuable Selective Awareness sessions are those that are least structured.

Excerpts from Food Diaries

Many of those who have had Selective Awareness Therapy for weight loss find that their personal journals and food diaries are as important to them as the exercises themselves. Here are some typical comments recorded by those who have completed the first Selective Awareness weight loss exercise:

I feel like I'm in contact with my body for the first time in my life. Now I *know* I can change.

I always thought losing weight was just a matter of eating less, and I never could do it. Now I know that my weight problem is all tied up with every other part of my life, not just the refrigerator.

I can't wait to start exercising again. Now I remember what a pleasure it is to get really physically tired and just feel that fat melting off.

When I remember how I ate that day, I could actually feel the chemicals being released into my body. I was really nervous, and it was like all those chemicals rushed right to my stomach and left a big hole there.

Food as Consolation

The following excerpt is from the food diary of a 27-year-old woman who had been overweight for about 15 years. When she finished the first Selective Awareness exercise for weight reduction, she found that she had gotten in touch with memories and feelings that had been buried for many years — since the death of her father, in fact, when she was 12 years old.

> On the day of father's funeral, I was very sick. My mother wouldn't let me go to the cemetery, she made me go to her friend's house instead, and this woman that was supposed to be taking care of me, she wouldn't let me cry. I was really sick, I felt like my stomach was turning inside out. And then there was a warning circle, right in the solar plexus, a black painful hole, squeezing tighter and tighter, and expanding at the same time, like it could just take me over. And it's never left me, there's always this black hole right there with me, in my stomach, and I have to keep it full of food. That's scary!
>
> This woman that I had to stay with, she had a box of candy in her living room, on the coffee table, and that night I sneaked into the living room and took that box of candy back into the room where I was sleeping, and I ate the whole thing in the dark. The dark outside and the dark inside were just like the same thing.

Moira wrote several pages about this experience when her father died. It seems that her mother had collapsed at the cemetery and had spent two days in the hospital. Although Moira was allowed to visit her, that wasn't exactly reassuring! The woman with whom Moira stayed, her mother's best friend, was also quite upset and unable to give Moira the love and reassurance she so desperately required. In fact, the friend apparently was afraid of expressing any emotion, of allowing Moira any kind of healthy release. Moira not only *felt* abandoned, she *was* abandoned, and in a particularly cruel way, by the death and illness of her parents and the emotional incapacity of her guardian.

Although she had completely "forgotten" these traumatic circumstances, Moira was able in her notebook to reconstruct how those feelings of abandonment, loneliness, and fear, and her subsequent reliance on food for comfort, had affected all her relationships since the age of 12. Through image rehearsal in Selective Awareness, she was able to draw upon this new understanding to retrain her mind and body to appreciate food without letting the need for emotional consolation rule her life.

As she wrote in her notebook, "Food will always be my friend — I love to eat. But it doesn't have to be my *only* friend. I'm going to find some human friends too. I'm going to let people get to know me, for the first time since I was a little kid."

Not all case histories are as clear and dramatic as Moira's. But it is common in Selective Awareness Therapy to become aware of feelings of loneliness, rejection, or despair. Remember, while there is no need to *relive* these feelings, getting in touch with them helps you to understand and accept them as part of what makes you uniquely and personally *you*.

Don't Let Your Feelings Own You

In the next Selective Awareness exercise you will learn to send specific messages of energy and reassurance to those parts of your body that have been tuned out. The goal is to form a total body link, a network of awareness, so that you can get in touch with any part of your body you choose. By rehearsing a complete meal, you will learn to break your old eating patterns and to eat sensibly and well, enjoying your food more than ever before.

In Selective Awareness Therapy, many realize that they feel compelled to overeat because of early conditioning in the form of statements such as: "It's a sin to waste food," "Think of all the children starving in India this very minute," and "You can't have dessert until you eat every bite on that plate." If you find such considerations influencing *your* eating habits, ask yourself if they need to continue doing so. Is it a greater sin to waste food by throwing it away, or to waste food by stuffing it into your body when you don't really need or want it?

By relying on your ideomotor finger signals to let you know where energy and attention are needed, you can help your body to break up fatty deposits. Many overweight people have actually rejected their whole bodies, so don't worry if you get a lot of negative feedback at first. This is information, and you can work with it.

Owning Your Own Feelings — Practice

(Use your preferred method for getting into the state of Selective Awareness.)

When you are deeply into the state of Selective Awareness, allow your "Yes" finger to lift.

Now orient back to a time when you felt really good, when you felt in touch with all of yourself, when your mind and body were working together in harmony. When you are there, let your "Yes" finger lift.

Is it OK to feel like that again? Is it all right to make those good feelings a permanent part of yourself? Allow your "Yes" finger to acknowledge the feeling of well-being as you realize that those positive feelings are yours, a part of you. If you felt good a couple of weeks ago you can feel good again today. As that familiar feeling of well-being returns, ask yourself if it is all right to consider change in a positive direction. Let yourself consider change in habit patterns, change in attitude, change in self-acceptance. When your "Yes" finger signals consent, see those changes clearly. Feel the power and security of greater self-acceptance. And as you feel that positive change, let your "Yes" finger lift again.

Now let yourself realize that attitudes and feelings are something you own, not something given to you by other people, and that you have the choice of accepting positive feelings and attitudes about yourself. And now take that option, take that choice, and own the feeling of well-being, of self-acceptance. Allow all your negative attitudes and emotions about yourself to drain away, and fill that empty space they leave with a feeling of confidence and security. Start with that feeling, let it expand and fill your body, filling all the places where you've been out of touch with yourself.

Now ask yourself if it would be all right to let that feeling of well-being continue, to stay with you as a permanent part of your self-awareness. As you find yourself even more relaxed, get in touch with the parts of your body that need help in receiving energy and attention. Let that awareness be total, be completely in touch with your body and its needs.

Reach inside yourself, get in touch with all the parts of your body that need a little help, until you become aware that you are reaching and incorporating all of yourself, for yourself. Imagine that you can look inside and become aware of how your body functions, involving all your body's processes in sending healing energy and awareness to wherever they are needed.

Now you can see the deposits of fatty tissue being absorbed, giving you a tremendous sense of well-being and control. Every time you get in touch with a part of your body that you have been disregarding, let that give you a feeling of well-being and confidence. Imagine that with this feeling of confidence you are looking in the mirror, acknowledging yourself, realizing that you can change the image in the direction of health.

As you look at your face in the mirror, notice your expression of relaxation, tranquility, and well-being and allow yourself to understand that you are on the road to self- acceptance and self-esteem, to getting in touch with your body, and doing what it needs. Allow yourself to feel the strength of wholeness.

Now project yourself forward in time, to a week from now. See yourself clearly in your favorite restaurant, relaxed and comfortable and confident, having a great time sharing yourself with your friends.

Imagine yourself looking over the menu and picking out something sensible, without being overly concerned — because what you eat is your choice. See yourself making that choice easily, with confidence. Now imagine the waiter bringing the appetizers. Help yourself to a nibble. As you eat slowly, enjoying your food, look around the restaurant; see if you notice others already halfway through their dinner who may not even be tasting it because they're eating so fast. Allow yourself to feel comfortable and secure because you know that this is not going to happen to you.

Now imagine that your soup has arrived. See yourself sipping a spoonful, tasting it, and enjoying it rather than filling yourself up. Notice how good it feels to realize that you can decide how much you want to eat and quit whenever you choose. When your salad is served, taste it, enjoy it, and allow yourself to realize when you've had enough.

As you imagine that your main course has arrived, become aware of how it looks, how it smells — allow yourself to enjoy the sight and smell of good food, well prepared. Allow yourself to feel joy and confidence as you realize that you don't have to live on grapefruit and skim milk in order to lose weight. And now as you take your first small bite, chew it slowly and well. And when you are just about ready to swallow it, chew it some more. Put your fork down and imagine looking around the restaurant until you see some overweight person staring at an empty plate or finishing the dessert his neighbor didn't have room for.

Now see yourself picking up the fork and having another bite and really enjoying the taste and texture of the food. Notice the sense of fulfillment you get from enjoying a good meal. If you find that you want a bite of dessert you might share it with someone, or order your own and have only a bite or two. Or you might skip dessert entirely. It's your choice.

When you are finished eating, when it's time to say, "OK, that's enough," see yourself crossing your knife and fork, or shoving your plate back, or some other gesture symbolic of having finished eating. Notice the sense of relief, the sense of freedom that comes from being able to choose to quit whenever you've had enough. When you realize that you really can choose to enjoy your food by simply listening to what your body tells you, let your "Yes" finger lift.

Now, as you count from one to five and return to a state of Social Awareness, allow yourself to feel relaxed and comfortable with your new knowledge, understanding that you can choose to eat sensibly and with even greater enjoyment than ever before.

(Count from one to five and return to the state of Social Awareness.)

Reward Yourself with Confidence — not with Candy

When you've lost your first few pounds through Selective Awareness Therapy, give yourself some positive feedback. Be sure to include all the positive elements of your progress, not just how much weight you've lost. Congratulate yourself on how much better you feel about yourself in general, as well as on your new acceptance of your body. Let yourself feel proud, and fully experience the corresponding emotional satisfaction as your self- image improves. And be sure to continue rehearsing that image of yourself as you're going to look — self-confident, vibrant, energetic, *and slim.*

One of the nicest kinds of positive feedback is to give your-self a present of a new dress or shirt, some new clothing that will reinforce your new image of yourself, looking and feeling your best.

Nine

Enjoy Freedom from Smoking

Most people who smoke *need* to smoke — for the moment, at least. Smoking is an oral habit, a source of gratification — it feels good to have something in your mouth, to let the smoke trickle down your throat, to feel the cigarette in your fingers. For most smokers, cigarettes are a continuation of a lifelong pattern of oral needs, progressing from mother's breast to bottle, pacifier, thumb, chewing gum, cigarettes, fingernails, and sometimes to drugs. Oral satisfaction is particularly important in times of stress, when you're nervous or uptight.

The first step in getting rid of the tobacco habit is to find out why you smoke. What kind of satisfaction do you get from cigarettes? Are you receiving emotional satisfaction, or are you acting out a self-destructive tendency? Why did you start to smoke, and why do you continue? Picture in your mind what smoking does to you not only in terms of health but socially, in terms of human relationships.

Smoking introduces tar into the lungs, making the pink, healthy lung tissue as dirty as a greasy old rag. Tobacco smoke affects the blood vessels, arteries, and heart, and it leads to premature aging. Nicotine affects your body chemistry, and tar damages the lung structures. Smoke is an irritant. It irritates the mucosal membranes of your nose, mouth, throat, and lungs, leading to chronic congestion, and sometimes to emphysema or cancer. The poisons in tobacco smoke can cause stomach problems and will contribute to arteriosclerotic heart disease. There is also evidence that smoking accelerates the aging process, causing wrinkled skin, dry, brittle hair, and hardened arteries.

But you already know all that. You know how you feel when

you wake up in the morning, you know how your mouth tastes, and you know that when you exercise, your lungs give out before your legs do.

You're also aware of the social consequences of smoking. You have only five senses with which to relate to other people, and when you smoke you extinguish two of them. You also deprive others of their sense of smell and to some extent of their sense of taste. And anyone who cares about you isn't going to enjoy watching you smoke, so you're depriving that person of three of five senses.

The odor of stale cigarette smoke has a way of hanging on that is atrocious to a nonsmoker. You really make nonsmokers vulnerable to your habit, and there's not very much they can do about it.

Remember, too, that children learn by imitation: they see you do something and they copy it. Is there a child in your family? Do you want to be responsible for that child's beginning to smoke?

You Don't Have to Substitute

One common fallacy that smokers rely on to perpetuate their habit is that if they quit smoking they'll eat more and gain weight. But using food to substitute for tobacco demonstrates only that the smoker hasn't yet worked out the dynamics of smoking. If you address the emotional component of the smoking habit, you won't need to compensate with greater quantities of food. In fact, you might even eat less: because food tastes so much better, your taste buds will be more easily satisfied.

When you quit smoking, you'll find that a whole world will open up — a new world of tastes and smells. Imagine for a moment that you are walking through a meadow in springtime. The flowers are out, and you can smell their fragrance — something you can't do when you're smoking because then all you can smell is the smoke.

Think for a moment of the situations you have exposed yourself to in perpetuating your smoking habit. Think of going out in a rainstorm to buy a pack of cigarettes. Or enduring the harsh looks of nonsmokers when you light up in a restaurant. Once you've quit smoking, you'll inevitably find yourself looking around for "safe" places to be, safe from the pollution of tobacco smoke. At times you may even appear self-righteous. But that's all right. The problems of not smoking are a joy compared to those of remaining enslaved to a habit you don't really want or need.

Of course, you do get *something* positive out of smoking, or you wouldn't have started in the first place or continued this long. When you decide to quit smoking through Selective Awareness Therapy, the first step is to become aware of all your reasons *for* smoking. So get out your notebook, and write down all the positive things you can think of about smoking — the physical and emotional satisfactions and release of nervous tension. Does smoking help you concentrate? Is the cigarette in your hand a valued social crutch in awkward situations? Is lighting up a little treat or reward you give yourself?

When you've written down everything positive, try it from the other angle — write down everything that's negative about smoking. That shouldn't be too difficult. Write down anything that comes up about why you smoke — why you started, when you are most likely to smoke too much, your feelings about the habit. Pay particular attention to anything that comes up about your fear of quitting.

Tobacco smoking is a tenacious habit, but it's one you *can* break. And just think how pleased you'll feel when you go for a hike and your legs give out before your lungs do, when you wake up in the morning with your nose and lungs clean and clear instead of clogged-up and aching.

Getting Ready

In giving up smoking through Selective Awareness Therapy you will practice two exercises. The first will help you to understand your smoking dynamics, to become fully aware of how wonderful it would be to quit. The second is for that day when you wake up in the morning knowing, "Today's the day — I'm going to give up smoking today!" Do the first exercise for as many days as you need to prepare yourself for *the* day. Modify the practice, if you like, to take into account your new understanding of your smoking habits. And there are several other things you can do to make that preparation easier.

First, make your cigarettes less accessible. If they're sitting right out there on your desk, you're likely to reach for one and light it out of habit, whether you want it or not. So put the pack in an unfamiliar place, like the bottom drawer of your desk; put your matches in another drawer, and your ashtray in yet a third place. That way you really have to think about what you're doing when you light a cigarette.

Second, you might try smoking even more than you usually do, until you're thoroughly sick of it and ready to quit.

Third, don't do anything else while you're smoking. Don't read, or watch TV, or talk to another person, or eat or drink anything. Particularly avoid smoking while you're drinking coffee or alcohol.

And fourth, don't *think* about anything else while you're smoking. Concentrate on what you're doing. Feel the effects of the smoke being drawn into your lungs and of the nicotine being carried through your blood stream. This may not be a pleasant experience, but it is enlightening to realize that this is what your body goes through every time you light a cigarette.

Throughout this chapter, reference is made to kicking the cigarette habit. If you want to give up smoking a pipe, or cigars, just substitute the appropriate words.

(If you are using a tape recording to help you get in touch with your smoking patterns, be sure to leave yourself enough time to go through the reviews given in the exercise.)

Understanding Your Smoking Patterns

(Use your preferred method for getting into the state of Selective Awareness.)

As your "Yes" finger signals that you are relaxed and comfortable in the state of Selective Awareness, take a deep breath, and as you let it out, let go of any areas of tension remaining in your body. Feel yourself drifting deeper into a state of peace and calm and healing, healing of body and mind.

Allow yourself to tune in to the rhythm of your breathing. Give your breath the importance it deserves. Feel yourself charged with energy as your lungs take in oxygen and discharge carbon dioxide, picking up positive feelings and emotions and letting go of tension. As you begin to feel that exchange, allow your "Yes" finger to signal affirmation.

Now ask yourself, "Would it be all right to evaluate my smoking habits, just to look at them and get in touch with them, with compassion and understanding?" When your "Yes" finger signals, allow yourself to go over in your mind a time when you really craved a cigarette. What are you feeling? What kind of satisfaction are you looking for? Are you feeling punitive toward yourself? When you become aware of what the feeling is, let your "Yes" finger signal, "Yes, that's what it is." Now view this need to smoke with sympathy and compassion, and ask yourself if smoking really gives you the gratification you're looking for.

Let your imagination review all the misery and embarrassment you put yourself through with your smoking habit. Imagine yourself going out in the rain to buy a pack of cigarettes. Imagine yourself bumming a cigarette, or lighting a half-smoked butt.

Think about the health hazards of smoking — the damage that smoking does to your lungs, and to your arteries, and the premature aging caused by damage to the arteries. Become aware of the example you set for other people, for children, maybe your own, maybe someone else's. Think for a moment of the senses you abolish when you smoke — the sense of smell, for yourself and others, the sense of taste, the taste and stale odor of cigarette smoke.

As you review all of the negative things about smoking, there may be times of agreement when your "Yes" finger will move, and times of disagreement when your "No" finger moves. Pay attention to these self-communications, see what your inner self is telling you.

Now ask yourself, "Would it be all right to consider not smoking?" When your "Yes" finger signals affirmation, let yourself drift deeper and deeper, gaining more insight into your smoking habit and into the dynamics that cause you to smoke. Already you may have become filled with an ever-increasing desire to give up smoking.

Now imagine that you have quit, that you have kicked the cigarette habit. Envision a whole day, from morning to night, in which you don't smoke. Allow that feeling of freedom to be a reward, a reward that will be lasting and will increase and will improve day by day because you are filled with a sense of pride and achievement. You will find that this feeling of health and freedom will give you all the satisfaction that you get from smoking, except that this satisfaction will last and will continue to last, day after day.

Imagine yourself several months from now, looking over a period of not smoking. See yourself feeling good and healthy and strong. Let that feeling of strength flow throughout your body, and let your "Yes" finger signal again.

Now let yourself become aware of your breathing. Realize that your breath supplies you with energy and life and how important it is that this energy be unpolluted and unadulterated. Follow the next few breaths and allow each breath to give you a feeling of well-being and energy that spreads throughout your entire body, to every part of your body, until you are filled with energy and with a sense of achievement and pride.

When you have thoroughly enjoyed your nonsmoking image, count from one to five and return to the state of Social Awareness, retaining the knowledge of how it feels to be a nonsmoker.

When you've firmly grasped the dynamics of your smoking habit and feel that your old patterns have weakened somewhat, it's time to quit. Let that day mature naturally; avoid setting a deadline. When the day arrives, read the following exercise carefully, and make any modifications that you feel will be useful based on your experience with the previous exercise and with your notebook.

Giving It Up

(Use your preferred method for getting into the state of Selective Awareness.)

Now take a deep breath and let yourself become aware of the importance of breathing, not only in terms of picking up energy and oxygen but symbolically as well. Breathe a deep breath with joy and exhale with a sigh, picking up good feelings and emotions and letting go of tension and negative feelings so that breathing can become a process of pleasure and of energizing.

Imagine that you are breathing not only into your lungs but all the way through your body, letting the joy of breathing take over as a natural rhythm, a wave of energy throughout your body. And think how nice it will be when that wave is clean and pure, unpolluted with tobacco smoke.

When you are ready, allow your mind to orient back to a time when you did something to perpetuate your smoking habit that was inconsistent with your true values. Review with compassion and understanding some of the unpleasant situations you have inflicted on yourself for the sake of a cigarette. And allow yourself to recognize the possibility of change, the possibility of a new way to go.

When your "Yes" finger signals recognition of the desire to change, imagine that the day has come when your reasons for smoking are no longer valid. As you feel an increasing desire to be free of cigarettes, tell yourself that soon you will know, "Today is the day." Imagine yourself getting up in the morning, knowing that today is the day when you will not smoke. As you imagine waking up on that morning, let your "Yes" finger move to reaffirm the knowledge that, "Today is the day." Now imagine going through an entire day without smoking, from morning to night. Notice how good it feels to have the choice of not smoking.

Now imagine that you are in a setting where you know you would have smoked before — having a cup of coffee after breakfast, perhaps, or working at your desk, or sipping a glass of wine after dinner. In your mind you may even reach out to get a cigarette when suddenly you realize, "No more! I'm a nonsmoker. I'm a nonsmoker!" And as you become aware of the significance of being a nonsmoker, you feel a tremendous sensation of reward, appreciation, almost as though someone is giving you a pat on the back, telling you, "Well done!" Imagine that you feel that reward now, so strongly that your "Yes" finger moves, reaffirming the feeling of strength and pleasure that you get from not smoking.

Now go over in your mind how many cigarettes you have been smoking every day. Imagine that instead of 20 cigarettes, or 30, you receive 20 or 30 pats on the back, congratulating you and rewarding you for not smoking. Soon you will find that the pleasure and strength and affirmation you receive will totally replace any of the satisfactions you may have been getting from smoking.

Once again, allow your mind to review a whole day without smoking, and feel that sense of achievement and relaxation and reward for every cigarette you might have smoked during that day. As your "Yes" finger acknowledges each one of these rewards, imagine the tremendous sense of accomplishment you feel at taking control of your life by not smoking.

Now see yourself going to bed that night, still with that tremendous rewarding sense of accomplishment, and waking up in the morning feeling better, cleaner, and more healthy than you have for years. Picture your lungs as you wake up in the morning as a nonsmoker. Imagine that your body is hard at work, healing and rejuvenating, replacing that old, blackened lung tissue with fresh, pink, healthy tissue that can do its job of taking in oxygen and energy better than ever. And just imagine that your lungs are thanking you for not smoking, your mouth and throat are thanking you for not smoking, your whole body is thanking you for not smoking.

Now imagine not smoking for a longer period of time, a

week, or a month, or a whole year of clean air — it's almost like a new life as your body rejuvenates itself, as your sense of smell and your sense of taste return.

When you have thoroughly enjoyed your new status as a non- smoker, count from one to five and return to the state of Social Awareness.

For a few people, it may take about three days after quitting for some of the poisons of tobacco smoke to be cleaned out of the body. If you are one of those people, you may experience some mild physical symptoms during those first few days, or you may feel slightly more nervous than usual. Welcome these symptoms as signs that your body is ridding itself of poisons and that energy is flowing through your body with renewed vigor. And remember to give yourself that reward, that pat on the back, 20 or 30 times a day.

Be gentle with yourself during this period. If you do have a relapse, now or at any time in the future, welcome it as an indication of something unresolved, something that still needs to be worked out in Selective Awareness. In that case, you can use your own modification of the tape for getting in touch with your smoking patterns, to help you understand your relapse.

Just remember not to be punitive with yourself and to allow yourself the freedom to do what is best for you.

When you have actually been a nonsmoker for a whole week, it's time to give yourself positive feedback. This will be similar to the last time — except that you can use your memory and your current experience instead of your imagination in describing how wonderful it is to be a nonsmoker. Allow yourself to experience fully the satisfaction and pride you take in your new freedom. Because you really have done something to be proud of!

Ten

Self-Image and Breast Development

I once delivered a paper on the subject of breast development to the Department of Neuropsychiatry at the University of California at Los Angeles. I didn't realize at the time how many problems this was going to create for me. The popular press picked up the story, and this one limited aspect of Selective Awareness Therapy became the subject of numerous newspaper and magazine articles. I was invited for interviews and guest appearances on radio and television shows — it seems that breast development is a subject of great popular interest. While all this attention was in some ways rewarding, it also was a bit upsetting because it tended to distort the real focus of my work, the use of Selective Awareness Therapy to help people achieve harmony of mind and body.

My interest in working with breast rejuvenation and growth began when some friends and I attended a night club performance by one of the world's greatest trumpeters. The trumpeter was in the middle of a set when a practical joker sitting at a table directly in front of the stage began to suck on a lemon. Within a few moments the musician had to retire from the stage because of the excessive salivation caused by watching that fellow sucking on a lemon.

My friends and I discussed the incident, and I explained how visual and other stimuli can cause different bodily organs to operate or activate glandular functions. One of the women at our table asked, "Would it be possible for the breasts, or other parts of the body, to grow after one has reached adulthood?" And I began to think about her question, to speculate on the possibilities of organ growth through mental stimulation.

I then decided to study the possibility of enhancing breast development through Selective Awareness Therapy. The first group I worked with consisted of 25 women who were concerned with the size of their breasts, who felt psychologically handicapped by their lack of development. Therapy extended over a ten-week period, with a one-hour session each week. Each woman made a tape recording for herself and played it daily.

By the end of the tenth week, 20 of the 25 women in the experimental group had experienced a measurable increase in the size of their breasts, and all but two felt happier and more comfortable with their bodies than they ever had before. Of course, these women volunteered for the study because they were concerned about their lack of development, to the point of great emotional suffering.

In working with cases of delayed breast development through Selective Awareness Therapy, one assumes that the cause is a "trauma" occurring in the formative years of life. As we have seen, thought, emotion, and behavior all affect the biochemical balance, which may in turn interfere with the growth and developmental processes of the body, including the breasts.

In cases where normal breast development fails to occur, the original trauma is frequently a matter of family identification and expectation. Or sometimes misinterpretation of a religious orientation toward the body creates a cycle of guilt and punishment that actually affects physical development.

The most common types of trauma resulting in underdevelopment of the breasts, in order of frequency, are:

1. Family identification, particularly with the mother
2. Social and religious misinformation
3. Male identification through upbringing
4. Teasing by family members or friends
5. Guilt from sexual play, including masturbation
6. Comparison with schoolmates and friends of the same age
7. Incestual encounters.

Whatever the reason for the initial trauma, the result is distortion of sensory input with negative feedback, establishing a self-fulfilling prophecy about the development of the body. (As stated by the Law of Sensitization, a sensitized person will distort incoming messages to confirm the validity of his or her sensitization.) The individual may avoid looking at herself in the mirror and refuse to participate in physical activities such as swimming or dancing. Most of the women in my original study, for example, censored tactile input rather severely. Many of them avoided having their breasts touched during sexual contact and reported unpleasant sensations when their breasts were touched. Body assessments in Selective Awareness revealed blank areas in the awareness of the breasts, and thermal evaluation using very sensitive thermometers revealed temperature differences of as much as 20 degrees between the breasts and surrounding areas of the body. Such drastically lowered temperature is a tangible sign of severe energy depletion in the affected area.

Several of the women who sought therapy appeared fully developed, some even overdeveloped. These women were the victims of an exaggerated social expectation. "If big is good, then bigger is better!"

Obviously, not every woman who is small-breasted wants to change. The following two Selective Awareness exercises can be modified to get further in touch with your own body and to enhance your appreciation and awareness of yourself. The first is a simple exercise designed for getting in touch with your breasts in a pleasant, positive way. The second is an exploration of the dynamics of this area of the body and further in-depth image rehearsal.

Before you begin the exercise, spend a little time getting in touch with your conscious feelings about your breasts. Get out your notebook and write down everything that comes into your mind about this area of your body. Then you will want to explore your feelings in the state of Selective Awareness. If you do that, remember to use the system of consider, consult, and consent, and pay attention to the information you receive from your ideomotor finger signals.

And every time you do one of the exercises, be sure to write down everything you've learned in that session, even if it's only a few brief notes.

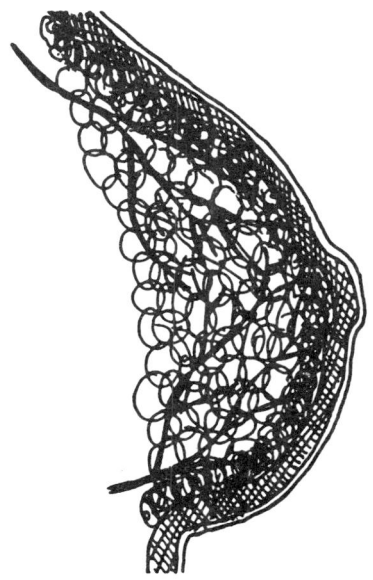

Profile of Breast

Getting in Touch with Your Breasts

(Use the method you prefer for getting into the state of Selective Awareness.)

When you are completely relaxed in the state of Selective Awareness, let your "Yes" finger lift and allow that motion to carry you even deeper, to deepen your sense of relaxation about yourself and your body.

Now ask yourself, "Would it be all right to get in touch with my breasts, to send them the energy and attention they deserve?" When your "Yes" finger signals affirmation, let yourself become aware of your breasts, aware that they are a very important part of your body. See that your breasts have been like a plant shaded from the sun, not getting the warmth and attention they need. Let yourself become aware of that spot in the center of your body that is the center of physical energy and allow that energy to spread up into both breasts. As you feel that energy spreading up through your body, let your "Yes" finger signal your increased awareness of your breasts, a pleasant awareness, a flow of warmth and energy. Let that energy fill you until you find that your breasts are absorbing all of your attention.

Now allow your breasts to be involved with the rest of your body in a new way. Imagine that you are touching them and that they are being touched. Become aware of yourself, appreciating and accepting yourself. As you accept that warmth and awareness, you will find that you are feeling more confident about yourself, more at ease with yourself than ever before.

Imagine yourself now as you would like to look, not just your breasts but your whole body. Be realistic, see yourself as you *can* look, at your best, receiving comfortable, positive, pleasurable feedback from your whole body. And notice a pleasant sense of awareness of your breasts as warmth and energy flow into them.

When that image of yourself is firm in your mind, let your "Yes" finger lift again. And remember that as you accept yourself and appreciate yourself, you get closer and closer to wholeness, to harmony of mind and body. Let that understanding give you a good feeling about yourself. As you count from one to five and return to the state of Social Awareness, retain that feeling of tranquility, well-being, and a sort of hidden excitement about yourself.

(Count from one to five and return to the state of Social Awareness, using the words and images that you prefer.)

Developing Your Breasts

(Go into the state of Selective Awareness, using the method you prefer.)

When your "Yes" finger signals that you are deep in the state of Selective Awareness, relaxed and comfortable, all your muscles limp and loose and relaxed, allow yourself to have a fantasy of yourself as you would like to look. Let your fantasy create a picture of yourself, a very comfortable and assured picture. Concentrate on seeing your breasts as you'd like them to be. When that image is very clear and definite, allow your "Yes" finger to lift, signaling your mind to organize and mobilize the energy that is necessary for breast growth, realizing that breast growth is not limited to a specific time in your life. It can take place at any time. Allow your fantasy image and finger signals to cooperate, telling your body and mind to let that warmth and energy flow freely through your breasts.

Now let yourself become even more aware, concentrating particularly on your nipples. As you become aware of your nipples, let your "Yes" finger lift again, and enjoy this new awareness fully. Notice how comfortable this awareness of your nipples feels, and gradually allow this pleasant awareness to spread to the area around your nipples. As you get in closer and closer touch with that area, allow your "Yes" finger to signal your enjoyment of this loving, caressing, sensual awareness. Allow that sensation to spread to all of the skin that covers your breasts, giving you a wonderful, warm, glowing feeling.

Now let yourself become aware of the structure of your breasts, the breast tissue, the milk-producing glandular tissue, the fatty tissue that makes up the structure of your breasts. As you become aware of the wholeness of your breasts, let your "Yes" finger lift again, reinforcing your understanding and enjoyment of that wholeness.

And now visualize and feel the vascular structure of your breasts, a tree-like structure of blood vessels branching into smaller and smaller vessels, carrying blood and energy and warmth throughout your breasts. As you feel that warmth, as you visualize those blood vessels, let your "Yes" finger lift. Imagine those blood vessels expanding, bringing even more blood and oxygen and nutrients to the breasts. And as your blood vessels expand, the sensation of warmth and awareness increases, until you are even able to detect a pulse in your breasts. When that happens let your "Yes" finger move again. As your finger lifts, allow yourself to drift deeper, into deeper understanding of the dynamics of breast growth, so that it becomes part of your awareness, part of your everyday life.

Now allow yourself to see the cellular growth taking place, just as though you are watching it through a microscope. Notice the process of cellular division as one cell divides to produce two, and the two produce four. When this picture is clear and vivid let your "Yes" finger lift again.

Now ask yourself if it would be all right to allow yourself a pleasant fantasy, a fantasy in which you recognize your breasts as part of your sexual makeup, a part of you, very definitely female. When your "Yes" finger signals assent, allow yourself to go into an erotic fantasy, seeing your breasts as though they're being cupped, as though they're being caressed, kissed, and cared for. Give yourself plenty of time, and let your own fantasy take over.

When your fantasy is finished, let your "Yes" finger lift. Now take a deep breath, and let that breath flow directly into your breasts. Picture yourself standing straight and tall, with perfect posture. Feel a sense of pride about your entire body, and let that pride be an indication that you've accepted your breasts and are perfectly happy with them, as they are now and as they will be.

Take another deep breath, and as you are filled with the pleasure of breathing, concentrate on breathing into only one breast at a time. Let yourself become aware exclusively of your right breast, the nipple, the area around your nipple, the skin, the tissue underneath it, the blood vessels, the pulse. As soon as your "Yes" finger signals readiness, move on to the left breast. Let yourself become aware of it, let yourself become aware of your left breast, the nipple, the skin of the breast, the tissue underneath the skin, the pulsations of the blood vessels. When your "Yes" finger signals, allow yourself to become aware of your right breast and then your left breast, alternately, for as long a time as you like.

Finally, let yourself become aware of both breasts simultaneously, with a very pleasant and sensual awareness. Retain this awareness of your breasts as you count from one to five and return to the state of Social Awareness, feeling refreshed, relaxed, and comfortable.

Eleven

Learning How to Learn — And How to Take a Test

As we have seen, a great deal of learning takes place in the amnestic period of life, before conscious memory. Through Selective Awareness, we can get in touch with this material, proving that just because we don't remember learning something doesn't mean that we didn't learn it. The same thing is true for other kinds of learning, including the kind we do in school. All the material you have read and studied is there in your mind, whether you are consciously able to call it out or not. Taking a test in school, giving a report at work, or writing a paper is largely a matter of recalling and organizing the information that's already there in your mind; the problem is getting at it when you need it, in a form you can use.

Because the state of Selective Awareness is not bound by the rules of ordinary time, you can use it to compress and review a great deal of material very quickly. And through image rehearsal you can learn to be relaxed and comfortable about taking a test or presenting a report.

It is your ability to review the material you have learned that will allow you to master the test situation. In Selective Awareness you will learn to tune in to everything that you've read, learned, practiced, or heard in the classroom, in personal experience, or through any other medium. You will also learn a technique for taking in and assimilating new material.

When cortical activity is suppressed, as in the state of Selective Awareness, your ability to recall the learned material will be greater because the pathway of the information in your brain is more direct. In the following Selective Awareness exercises you will see yourself studying the material you want to learn. Then you will actually go ahead and study. When you have finished studying, you will go back into the state of Selective Awareness and quickly review what you've learned, so that in the future you will have easy access to that material.

It is frequently the case that anxiety about test-taking blocks access to the information that's needed. In the Selective Awareness exercise on test-taking, you will project forward to a testing situation, so that you can rehearse walking into the examination room with a sense of total security about your mastery of the subject.

In general, the material you learn through Selective Awareness is more permanently yours than what you've only read in a book or heard in the classroom. If it's at all possible, therefore, it's better not to study the night before an important test. Take the evening off and let your mind relax. Anxiety about a testing situation can effectively block access to the material that you *know* you know. So the more relaxed you are when you walk into the classroom, the better you will do — especially when your calm state of mind is based on confidence in your mastery of the material.

Improve Your Studying

The first step in learning to learn through Selective Awareness is to take a pencil and a piece of paper and make an outline of your previous exposures to the material you need to learn. Write down what you have learned not only from classroom instruction but from all other sources — parents, television, radio, newspapers, or travel. Give yourself a broad overview of what you already know. You will be surprised at the amount of material you didn't even know you knew. Get together all your books, notes, and any other equipment you will need — when it's time to study you won't want any interruptions.

Since most of the following exercise is silent review, you

may prefer not to make a tape for learning to study. Simply fix the instructions firmly in your mind, go into the state of Selective Awareness, and allow your mind to move through the exercise at its own speed.

When your "Yes" finger signals that you are deep in the state of Selective Awareness, count backward from ten to one and allow yourself to recall more and more information about the subject at hand. Let that information flow quickly and effortlessly through your mind. Each time a new bit of information falls into place, let your "Yes" finger lift, and each time it lifts more information will come in. Notice the feeling of increased confidence as you realize how much you already know and how much more information is coming in that you didn't know you knew. Repeat the countdown from ten to one until you are satisfied that the information is firmly in your mind.

Now imagine that you are sitting at your desk studying. See yourself studying with such concentration and pleasure that you know that the material will sink right into the memory center of your brain, ready to be recalled whenever you need it. When that image is clear and vivid in your mind, let your "Yes" finger lift, realizing as you count from one to five and return to the state of Social Awareness that everything you study will be firmly and properly placed in your memory center, ready for instant recall.

(Count from one to five and return to the state of Social Awareness.)

Now it's learning time. Sit down at your desk, or wherever you study, with a feeling of confidence in your ability to absorb all the material you need to learn. You will find yourself less distracted. Go ahead and finish your work, just as you did in your image rehearsal.

When you have finished studying, return to the state of Selective Awareness, and quickly review all of the material that's relevant to your test, particularly what you've just learned. As you count from ten to one, let all the information you've just learned become even more firmly embedded in your memory. Repeat this process as often as you like.

Breathe deeply, inhaling energy and exhaling tension and anxiety that might interfere with the smooth recall of information. Breathe easily and comfortably as you allow yourself to review all of the information that relates to the test you'll be taking. Scan the information quickly, allowing your "Yes" finger to confirm important points. Mentally see yourself sopping up information like a sponge, feel all that information flowing through your mind, without effort or tension.

Allow your "Yes" finger to signal when that review is complete, and return to the state of Social Awareness, feeling relaxed and comfortable and full of confidence.

Taking a Test

A few days before any important test, begin doing image rehearsals so that on the day of the test you can walk into the classroom with your mind clear, free of any anxiety that might hamper your performance. Continue doing the image rehearsal until your body and mind understand that there really is no reason for being anxious and uptight about taking a test, and that relaxation is a normal, natural state in which you will be able to function better than ever before.

(Go into the state of Selective Awareness by your preferred method.)

When your "Yes" finger signals that you are ready, allow yourself to project forward to the day of the test. See yourself in the classroom, looking and feeling comfortable, full of confidence, *knowing* that you know the material and that it's right there for you to use.

See yourself walking into the room with a smile on your face, breathing calmly, looking around, maybe seeing some anxious faces, recognizing that you don't have to be anxious. Let your "Yes" finger lift to acknowledge that feeling of confidence and relaxation, knowing that you will be able to recall everything you need to know.

Imagine that you are taking the test right now, writing down the answers or working the problems, confidently and without hesitation. Imagine that you have finished the test. Hand in your paper, and as you leave the room, allow yourself to feel very proud of the job you have done.

When you have fully enjoyed the image of yourself having successfully completed the test, allow your "Yes" finger to signal affirmation of that feeling.

Now count from one to five and return to the state of Social Awareness with a feeling of tremendous well-being and confidence.

Twelve

Insomnia

As you have seen throughout this book, you have a great deal more control over body and mind than you usually give yourself credit for. But when you don't recognize that control, or work on developing it, the lack of mind-body harmony may manifest itself as the inability to sleep. Insomnia is frequently caused by misplaced and poorly timed attempts at problem-solving — you can easily get into the habit of lying awake and mulling over what's wrong with your life, instead of going to sleep.

In order to change your sleeping habits — or in the case of insomnia, your non-sleeping habits — it's helpful to know something about the dynamics of sleep.

Stages of Sleep

Even though most of us spend about a third of our lives asleep, only in the past ten years or so has this state of consciousness begun to be understood by physicians, psychologists, and other researchers. Recent experimentation has focused on the two basic sleep states, Rapid Eye Movement (REM) sleep and Non-rapid Eye Movement (NREM) sleep, and on the effects of drugs, particularly sleeping pills, on the central nervous system.

REM sleep is the normal phase of the sleep cycle that begins approximately 60 to 90 minutes after falling asleep and reoccurs in cycles of 20 minutes three to four times during the night. Most but not all dream activity takes place in this phase.

During REM sleep there is pronounced cerebral activity, while voluntary muscular movements, except eye movements, are inhibited. (The occasional eye flutter you may experience while slipping into the state of Selective Awareness is similar to REM activity and represents a similar discharge of tension.) The heart and lungs frequently show irregular rhythms.

REM sleep is the dream phase of sleep, during which all of the collected static and tensions of the day are discharged, so that you wake up rested and refreshed. When REM sleep is suppressed, emotional tension is not relieved, and even though your body may be rested after eight full hours in bed, your mind is not.

There are four stages of Non-rapid Eye Movement sleep, as measured by brain wave activity. The cycle of NREM-REM sleep is repeated from four to six times each night, with REM sleep occupying 20 to 25 percent of the total sleeping time. A greater amount of voluntary muscular activity takes place during NREM sleep than during REM sleep.

Causes of Insomnia

By far the most common cause of insomnia is anxiety over the seemingly insoluble problems of daily life. And of course if you haven't slept much, your problems seem that much worse the next day. When the preoccupations of the day interfere with sleep at night, the result may be the triple threat of insomnia, anxiety, and depression. At that point it's impossible to tell which condition is the cause and which the effect, since each contributes to the others.

Another fairly common form of sleep disturbance is pseudo- insomnia, in which a person's report that he "hasn't slept a wink" is contradicted by laboratory observation or by the reports of bed-partners. This condition is sometimes due to persistent dreams of being awake in bed, tossing and turning with insomnia.

Another variety of sleep disorder is an occasional disturbance of the circadian rhythm, the 24-hour rhythm of the body based on the cycle of day and night. A person may have a 26-hour biological rhythm, or internal clock, and a 24-hour day. This discrepancy may be reflected in the cyclic inability to sleep.

Insomnia sometimes has an iatrogenic basis. Once labeled "insomniac," a person may easily come to believe that he just cannot get to sleep without taking a pill. This negative suggestion that "You can't make it on your own" may soon build into a drug dependency which in itself leads to insomnia.

One of the most important things that can be said about insomnia is very simple: it doesn't matter whether you sleep or not. Lack of sleep has no ill effects on the body — a fact substantiated by Dr. William Dement at the Stanford Sleep Disorders Clinic and Laboratory.

If you get very little sleep one night, you'll be tired the next day and perhaps not able to function too well. But that's equally true if you've taken a sleeping pill. And if you're *really* tired, you'll be much more likely to sleep soundly the next night. Many people are labeled insomniacs when the truth is that they actually need less sleep than the average eight hours a night. Once they recognize this fact, they are delighted to make constructive use of the extra time, rather than lying in bed tossing and turning and fretting over "lost" sleep.

Insomnia and Drugs

If your sleepless state is disturbing enough to you, you may go to the doctor and ask for something to help you sleep. If you go to one who isn't up on the latest medication you may end up with a barbiturate, the most common type of sleeping pill. They're called "downers," and that's exactly what they are. Barbiturates deprive the body of REM sleep.

REM deprivation is characterized by tiredness and depression in the morning, despite a full night's sleep. And if your body and mind are deprived of REM sleep for even a relatively short time — say four or five nights of sleeping pills — then you may end up depressed and anxious because your brain is full of undischarged "static." It frequently happens that this kind of depression is treated with "uppers," perhaps in the category of amphetamines. Unfortunately, these drugs also have REM- suppressing qualities, leading to even greater levels of nervous tension and anxiety. If this condition is treated with tranquilizers, which also suppress REM activity, the picture of drug-induced insomnia, anxiety, and depression is complete.

Another problem with all kinds of "uppers" and "downers" is that their effects begin to wear off after a week or so, so that you have to take more and more pills to get the same effect.

All barbiturates deprive the brain of REM sleep, and so does another popular drug, alcohol. These two types of drugs, taken together, "potentiate" one another, or enhance each other's effects. That's why they're such a deadly combination. The effect is actually anesthetic, almost a chemical coma, so that there's really no chance at all of either body or mind being rested or refreshed by sleep.

When a patient comes to me with insomnia, the first thing I do is ask him to bring in all the medication he's been taking. It frequently happens that the person has been to more than one doctor and that each one has prescribed a different and perhaps contradictory drug. When the effects of each drug, taken separately and in combination, are reviewed and explained, many are astonished and at the same time relieved to understand that their symptoms are actually drug-induced.

Working with Insomnia

When you begin to work with insomnia in Selective Awareness Therapy, it's important to get rid of the labels "insomnia" and "insomniac," which imply that you won't be able to sleep no matter what you do. What you actually have is a temporary sleep disorder.

The first step is to take out your notebook and write down a review of your usual activities before going to bed. You may discover that this period is overloaded with stimulating or even alarming activities such as paying bills or discussing family problems. Or you may even be in the habit of discussing problems in bed. Or perhaps you're going to bed too early, before you're ready to go to sleep. I once had an overweight patient who developed "insomnia" as she began to lose weight. It turned out that she was going to bed every night at nine o'clock, in order to stay away from the refrigerator. Then, she would lie there tossing and turning for two or three hours and oversleep the next morning. In her case, understimulation rather than overstimulation was the problem, and joining a bridge club turned out to be the solution.

If you find that the period before bedtime is anything but relaxing, try to allow yourself at least one hour, and preferably two, between any disturbing or stimulating activities and the time you go to bed.

Observe your natural rhythm of sleepiness and wakefulness, so that you don't miss the moment for the transition to bed and sleep.

If you sleep with someone else, ask that person for his or her impressions of your sleeping habits. You may find that you're getting more sleep than you thought.

In your notebook, record your intake of any drugs — especially coffee and alcohol. Even though alcohol is a depressant, it may keep you awake by stimulating emotional states of excitement. And if you remember your dreams, write them down too. Clues to the basis of insomnia are frequently hidden in dreams.

Once you have finished the self-evaluation process, you will have a better idea of how to correct your sleep disorder, especially if it's caused by obviously faulty pre-bedtime habits — such as two cups of coffee after dinner, or picking up an exciting novel every night after you're in bed. Correct any habits that are obviously self-defeating and designed to keep you awake. Organize your evenings so that you can relax, and just before you're ready to go to sleep, practice the following Selective Awareness exercise.

This exercise is designed to relieve sleeplessness caused by improper preparation for sleep. The following exercises will help with sleeplessness caused by anxiety and repetitive, futile attempts at problem-solving.

Since this exercise is short and straightforward, you may prefer not to make a tape, but simply to read it over, noting the important points, and then to go through it in the state of Selective Awareness.

Relaxing into Sleep

(Use your preferred method for getting into the state of Selective Awareness.)

When your "Yes" finger signals that you are relaxed and comfortable in the state of Selective Awareness, pretend that your eyelids are so heavy that you cannot open your eyes. Test your fantasy and notice how that act allows you to drift even deeper into relaxation of body and mind. Every time an unwanted thought comes into your mind, simply pretend that your eyelids are so heavy that you can't open your eyes, and allow the thought to leave your awareness.

Now imagine that you are getting ready for bed. See yourself doing all the things that you usually do, brushing your teeth, getting into your night clothes. See yourself preparing for bed quietly and efficiently, not worried or anxious about anything, but looking forward to climbing in between the sheets.

Now imagine that you are getting into bed. Turn out the lights, stretching and yawning because you are already very sleepy. Now, as you count back from ten to zero, see yourself falling asleep, quickly and comfortably, without worrying or thinking about anything in particular. As you continue to count back rehearse an entire night of deep, refreshing sleep, complete with periods of REM sleep and dreaming. As you reach the count of zero, see yourself waking up in the morning, refreshed, alert, and relaxed after a good night's sleep.

Now repeat the countdown again, as often as you like, until the feeling of deep, refreshing sleep becomes not only a possibility but something that your mind and body expect to happen when you go to bed.

When your internal mind is in agreement with the image of deep and restful sleep, let your "Yes" finger signal the strength of that connection.

When you have thoroughly enjoyed your image of a full night's sleep, count from one to five and return to the state of Social Awareness, completely relaxed and comfortable in mind and body, and ready for the real thing.

Practice this image rehearsal every night either just before or just after you go to bed, allowing the vision of yourself enjoying a sound sleep to replace the old pattern of worry and anxiety. If you practice when you're already in bed, don't bother to return to the state of Social Awareness — just let yourself drift on to sleep. After a few nights your sleep cycle will have readjusted itself. Every time you enter the state of Selective Awareness, your body and mind will copy some of the effects of REM sleep by discharging excess muscular and nervous tension, until your attitudes and habits of sleep have adjusted themselves to the new and healthy pattern.

If your sleeping difficulties persist after several evenings of Selective Awareness image rehearsal, explore the reasons for your sleeplessness. Go into the state of Selective Awareness, by whatever means you prefer, and orient back to a time when you had no trouble sleeping — when you literally slept like a baby. Use the system of consider, consult, and consent, and pay attention to the information you receive from your ideomotor finger signals. Now count back from ten to zero and allow your mind to come up to the time in your life when sleeping became difficult. Whenever you touch on a situation or event or state of mind that presented difficulty in sleeping, or that kept you awake or told your mind "alert, awake," allow your "Yes" finger to move. As your "Yes" finger signals, you will have flashes of insight that will allow you to understand this material, to understand what is keeping you awake.

Repeat this count from ten to zero as often as necessary to get all the information you need. When all that information is clear in your mind, when you understand what is preventing you from sleeping normally and naturally as you once did, then go back over it using image rehearsal to see yourself in each situation, sleeping well and soundly all night long.

When your image rehearsal is complete, repeat to yourself several times the words, "I deserve to sleep." What does your inner mind say in response to that? "I deserve to sleep. I deserve to sleep." Every time a thought occurs in response to that statement, acknowledge and accept it, and allow yourself to go on to the next response.

As soon as you return to the state of Social Awareness, write down everything you have learned, so that you can work with it in later sessions.

"I Deserve to Sleep"

Another exercise you can practice in Selective Awareness is to choose one hand to represent the part of you that wants to sleep, that deserves to sleep. Let the other hand represent the part of you that is not going to let you sleep, the insomnia hand. In Selective Awareness, imagine that your two hands are having a dialogue; begin by having the affirmative hand say, "I want to sleep." Put all your imagination into the opposing hand and listen to what it says.

This dialogue in Selective Awareness will often take you to the foundation of problems that are almost completely subconscious. When the dialogue is complete, ask yourself if these difficulties in sleeping need to persist, or if it would be all right to let go of them. With the consent of your inner mind, you can then return to the first exercise, and practice the image rehearsal for relaxing into sleep.

It is consoling to remember that lack of sleep is not harmful or damaging — the only drawback is that you're tired the next day. When you become convinced that nothing detrimental will happen if you lie awake for a couple of hours, you may risk getting rid of your sleeping pills. If you also abstain from drinking alcohol in the evening, your REM activity will return, and you will find that what sleep you do get is refreshing and rejuvenating.

Thirteen

Improving Your Sports Performance

Improving Your Golf Game

James, a professional golfer, came to me just before a major tournament with the complaint that he had not won a tournament in over two years. That isn't very good for the reputation or earnings of a professional golfer — in fact, it's downright bad! Exploration in the state of Selective Awareness revealed an attitude of "I don't care," an almost complete lack of motivation. As James reviewed the source of his problem, he stated that he was very depressed about his marital situation — he and his wife didn't enjoy being married to each other, but both found it convenient, since she was his booking agent and secretary. This attitude toward his marriage had seriously affected his golf game.

The first step in James' Selective Awareness Therapy was to separate his marital problems from his professional activity. Because time was so short — in fact, he was supposed to leave for the tournament the next morning — it was decided for the time being to concentrate on improving his golf game and to deal with the marital problems later.

In the state of Selective Awareness, James was asked to orient back to the last time he had won and to review that entire game. He was then asked to review all of the past games in which he had played well and to extract from each the most exceptional strokes. He thus ended up with a series of outstanding strokes. Next he was asked to create a synthetic game, using all of these exceptionally good strokes, and to then project them onto the course to be played in the tournament. This final image rehearsal, of seeing himself playing the synthetic game on the course to be played, was repeated several times, with the suggestion that his "Yes" finger would lift when he was completely comfortable with his new expectations. He was then asked to see himself in the winner's circle, receiving a prize.

On the first day of the tournament, James tied for second place. The next day, his early celebrations and excessive alcohol intake caused him to drop from second place to a slightly lower category, but he did finish fourth out of a field of over 100 — a position financially as well as emotionally rewarding.

After this tournament, James learned to make image-rehearsal and confidence-building tapes for himself. And by reviewing past games he was able to spot defects and errors in his technique. For example, he became aware that his upswing was rough and jerky. He related that problem to muscular tension in the back and shoulders caused by fear of not being able to perform well under the pressure of competition.

James and his wife did come back to work on their marital problems, and as a result, they are still together. In this case, simply recognizing the connection between the state of his marriage and his golf game was enough for James to separate the two problem areas, in order to work on them individually.

Becoming Number One

Tim was a college swimmer whose coach felt that he had a great deal of potential. The problem was that Tim almost always came in second, no matter what the competition.

In Selective Awareness, Tim was asked to visualize himself participating in the Olympic Games — to which he signaled "No." When asked to explain that "No," he said, "Of course I can't — I'm not that good." It became apparent that Tim had an image of himself as "second best."

Orienting back to his childhood, Tim saw himself on numerous occasions competing with his older brother and usually coming out second best. The older brother was an excellent swimmer, and Tim both admired and felt competitive toward him. The result was that he was never able to beat his brother, never better than "second best."

With this new understanding of his own motivations, Tim was asked to review several recent swim events in which he had done well. He had placed first only once, but had actually swum quite well in several of the events in which he had placed second.

As he reviewed his "second best" performances, Tim noticed some faults in his style and mentally corrected those errors through image rehearsal. After reviewing his most satisfactory event several times, Tim used image rehearsal to visualize several future events in which he imagined coming in first until he became familiar with the possibility of being Number One. He continued to review these future events until his "Yes" finger signaled that he was comfortable and familiar with the concept of winning.

The effects were dramatic. Tim became the Number One swimmer for his school, and many of the records he set still stand. Tim shared his knowledge of Selective Awareness techniques with other members of his team, and soon the divers as well as the swimmers were making Selective Awareness tapes to help them improve their performances. Another benefit reported by every member of the team was increased energy — they were able to practice longer between breaks and weren't tired out, even after competitions.

This kind of visualization and image rehearsal in Selective Awareness Therapy has been used effectively to improve performance in scuba diving, skiing, baseball, tennis, and archery, as well as swimming, diving, and golf. It is particularly effective in sports where eye-muscle coordination and unswerving concentration are important, such as tennis and archery.

Every summer I practice image rehearsal of my skiing technique, so that at the beginning of each season I ski just as well as I did at the close of the last one.

Improving Any Sports Performance

The following Selective Awareness exercise contains several parts. The first section is designed to help you get in touch with your centers of physical and mental energy, followed by an exercise for "recharging your batteries." The rest of the exercise is concerned with image rehearsals of yourself performing in your sport as you would like to perform and other image rehearsals that will enable you to do your best. You may wish to divide this exercise into two or three sessions, each concentrating on a particular aspect. Also, as you read the next few pages, notice the places where you will personalize the exercise by inserting details about your particular sport. This is especially important in the sections on image rehearsal.

To achieve the objectivity necessary to see the mistakes in your performance, you may find it helpful to visualize it on a movie or television screen, so that you can watch yourself as you would watch another person.

(Use your preferred method to go into the state of Selective Awareness.)

When your "Yes" finger signals that you are relaxed and comfortable in the state of Selective Awareness, take a deep breath; as you exhale allow any remaining areas of tension in your muscles to let go, so that you are completely and totally relaxed, from the top of your head right down to the tips of your toes.

As you breathe deeply and evenly, taking in not only oxygen but physical energy as well, feel that energy spreading throughout your body, energizing every muscle, tuning up your whole metabolism. Think of the food you eat, of how your body receives and stores energy from nourishment, so that you can call on it when you need to.

Now, as your body remains relaxed and comfortable, feel how it is charged with energy, energy available to be used whenever you call on it. Allow yourself to drift deeper and deeper into awareness of the energy potential within your body.

Count back from ten to zero, becoming even more aware of the physical energy stored in your body. (Count from ten to zero, using the words and images that are appropriate for you.) Now pretend that you cannot open your eyes, allowing that action to bring you in tune with the mental energy that is necessary for physical coordination. When you are in touch with the center of mental energy, allow your "Yes" finger to lift.

To bring the physical and mental energy centers into alignment, you will now go through a physical tune-up just as though you were charging your battery. Breathe deeply, realizing that breath is one of the sources of life energy. It is through breathing that we maintain life. As you breathe, realize that you are breathing in energy. See this energy not only being inhaled but also stored within you, just as energy is stored in a battery.

Allow yourself now to become aware of the center of your body, the center where energy is conserved for times of need. When your lungs take in oxygen, energy is stored. When your stomach and intestines absorb food and nutrients, energy is stored. When your liver produces glycogen from sugar, energy is stored. Picture your heart pumping energy into your blood stream. When you are fully in touch with the energy center of your body, picture that energy being released when you call upon it, see it flowing to every muscle, reenergizing your whole body. As you feel that surge of joyful energy, let your "Yes" finger lift.

Now let yourself become aware of your sports goals. Take as long as you like to rehearse those goals. Picture yourself performing in your sport as you would like to, full of confidence and energy and skill.

When your rehearsal is complete, allow your mind to review several situations or events in which you have done well in your sport, times when you played well and did your best. And ask yourself if it would be all right to take the best ingredients of each event in this review and project them into a future event. "Is it all right for me to take my best performances and create an image reflecting what I have been able to do or what I expect to be able to do?"

Now, as you count back from ten to zero, see yourself performing better and better within that framework of past success and with confidence in your future abilities — which may become limitless.

Be permissive with yourself, and realize that there are other people who are working just as hard as you to achieve the same goal. Even if someone out-performs you, you can use the experience to learn how to improve your next performance. You will find that the next time you are out on the golf course or the tennis court, you'll have a tremendous feeling of well-being and tranquility, which permits you to conserve energy for when it is needed.

Now rehearse that future event again. See yourself being very calm, very relaxed, immune to the comments of both spectators and other competitors.

Picture yourself physically and mentally calm, working with great economy of motion, using only the amount of energy you need, when you need it. Picture yourself conserving your energy until the proper moment and then unleashing it, just as though you had unzipped a bag full of pure energy. When this image is clear and vivid, allow your "Yes" finger to signal.

Now project yourself forward to a time after an event has taken place. See yourself feeling satisfied and proud of your performance, telling yourself that you have done a good job. And let that image give you such a tremendous feeling of well-being and satisfaction that you want to go out and practice as soon as you can.

As you count from one to five and return to the state of Social Awareness, allow yourself to retain that feeling of high energy, both physical and mental, and of satisfaction and well-being.

(Count from one to five and return to the state of Social Awareness.)

After your next successful game, event, or tournament, give yourself some positive feedback, adding to your image rehearsal anything new you've learned. Congratulate yourself on your energy and skill, and let yourself experience fully the joy and pride you take in playing your best game. Remember that the more positive feedback you give yourself, the greater your improvement will be. If you have made errors or failed in your performance, review it and learn from it — thereby turning failure into a positive learning experience.

If you are just learning a new sport, or taking lessons, you can combine the Selective Awareness exercise for learning with those for improving your sports performance. First, in the state of Selective Awareness, imagine that you are receiving a lesson. See yourself absorbing everything your instructor tells you or shows you. After you have actually had your lesson, go back into the state of Selective Awareness and review the lesson you've just received. And finally, use image rehearsal to practice everything you've just learned.

Fourteen

Healing After Surgery

Making Surgery and Recovery Easier

Mrs. Harrington came to me with an acutely infected gall bladder that had to be removed. She said, "Doctor, it can't be done. I'm allergic to anesthetics — I go into shock." She then told me that some years before she had been scheduled for surgery for a gynecological problem. Almost as soon as the procedure was begun, however, it had to be terminated because she went into shock. A month later surgery was attempted again, but no sooner was the incision made than she went into shock. Assuming that the shock was due to chemical anesthesia, the surgical team scheduled her for a third time; but this time Mrs. Harrington asked to remain awake and was given a spinal anesthetic. The surgery was successfully completed on that occasion. Unfortunately it would be impossible to remove a gall bladder using only a spinal anesthetic.

Since I knew that patients under anesthesia can still respond to meaningful stimuli, I considered the possibility that Mrs. Harrington's shock was psychogenic rather than due to anesthesia. I asked her if she would like to explore that possibility in Selective Awareness. She readily agreed and quickly learned to slip into the state of Selective Awareness.

After a few moments of exploration, she suddenly blurted out, "Oh, my God, I can hear Dr. Bird (the surgeon) saying to the anesthesiologist, 'You're so dumb, why don't you get the hell out of here and go back where you came from?'" Obviously it's a very meaningful stimulus for an anesthetized patient to realize that the man responsible for her anesthesia should, in the opinion of the surgeon, "get the hell out of here." And so she went into shock and from then on always went into shock following the administration of anesthesia.

I asked Mrs. Harrington if it would be all right for me to introduce her to my surgical team. She agreed, and when we met the nurses and the anesthesiologist and the surgical assistant with whom I would be working, she was quite reassured.

She and I then rehearsed in Selective Awareness all the steps leading up to the surgery, the surgery itself, and the postoperative recovery period.

The tape that she made for herself, after only two sessions in Selective Awareness, was quite inventive. She instructed herself, "Imagine for a moment that the nurse is coming in to tell you that you are ready for surgery, and let that be a cue to drift off and go hiking in the mountains. But you'll be there, too, in the hospital, able to respond to questions and aware of everything that's going on. And every time you are moved or lifted from a bed to a gurney, or whenever anybody asks you a question, that will be a cue to go into an even deeper, more comfortable state of Selective Awareness."

We rehearsed her waking up after the surgery feeling very comfortable, we rehearsed her eating her favorite meal so that her intestines could regain normal functioning as soon as possible, and we rehearsed her feeling so good that she might not have to have any injections for pain following the surgery.

(In fact, Mrs. Harrington felt so good after the surgery that she suggested to the nurse that she herself take the injection for pain; the nurse didn't understand and kept trying to administer the shot.)

During surgery, to test Mrs. Harrington's awareness under anesthesia, the anesthesiologist leaned over her and said into her ear, "Rumpelstiltskin." When I asked him why he had said that to her, he replied, "She's now at the greatest depths of surgical anesthesia. If she remembers that I'll believe that people can hear under anesthesia." That same day, after her operation, Mrs. Harrington asked the anesthesiologist, "Why did you say 'Rumpelstiltskin' to me during the surgery?"

It was from my experience with Mrs. Harrington that I became aware of the extreme importance of pre-operative preparation for postoperative recovery. All of Mrs. Harrington's functions returned to normal within a day of surgery. She was ambulatory and her bowels moved on the first day, and she was discharged on the third postoperative day.

Less than twenty hours after her surgery, I went to Mrs. Harrington's room to see her and was surprised to find that she wasn't there. Somewhat alarmed, I went looking for her. I finally found her at the snack bar, where she was happily devouring a hamburger and a milk shake. When she saw me, she burst into a huge grin and said, "Doctor, I feel wonderful. Anyone who hasn't had surgery like that has missed something in life!"

Making the Painful Comfortable

Walter Jesperson was a proper gentleman, 74 years of age, who required both a circumcision and a hemorrhoidectomy. To do both at the same time would be difficult but would lessen the shock to his system in terms of postoperative recovery time.

But because Mr. Jesperson was so very proper — and also so very neutral (he didn't say "yes," he didn't say "no," he was just there) — it became obvious that we would get nowhere unless we could rehearse every step of his surgeries and the postoperative recovery period. Whatever I said to this man he repeated back to me parrot-fashion; but until we decided to use Selective Awareness image rehearsal it seemed almost hopeless to continue with him because of his rigidity.

We rehearsed every step of the pre-operative procedures, the surgeries themselves, and most importantly, the postoperative recovery period. Still not realizing how literally this patient interpreted everything that was said to him, I suggested, "When I come to your room following surgery, you will have a tremendous urge to go to the bathroom."

We had no problems with the pre-operative procedures, and surgery was quite successful. He was able to move his bowels and to urinate within the first day after surgery. But when I went to his room to see him immediately after surgery, I had no sooner entered the room than he got out of bed, walked to the bathroom, turned around, walked back to his bed, and climbed into it. When I asked him what he was doing, he replied, "You told me that when I saw you enter my room I should feel a tremendous urge to go to the bathroom. That's what I did." But he did nothing more.

While Mr. Jesperson did recover fully and rapidly, his very literal interpretation of my suggestion made me realize that we can never assume that the doctor and the patient are necessarily talking about the same thing or understanding one another at all. This patient's primness and preciseness did not permit him to interpret "going to the bathroom" as including the actual functions of bowel movement and/or urination!

Shortening the Hospital Stay

There is an acute shortage of hospital beds in this country today, amounting almost to a crisis as the available hospital space and services lag behind the growing demand. One approach to this problem was reported in the *Journal of the American Medical Association* in an article entitled, "Experience with Shortened Hospital Stay for Postsurgical Patients."[1] This approach, which not only results in "instant" hospital beds but also has obvious benefits for the patient, is to substantially

---

[1] Arthur Innes, M.D.; Arline J. Grant, M.D.; and Malcolm S. Beinfield, M.D., "Experience with Shortened Hospital Stay for Postsurgical Patients." In *JAMA*, 204:8, May 20, 1968.

reduce the hospital stay whenever possible. In the study reported in this article, 200 unselected patients were able to shorten the customary period of postsurgical hospital convalescence by one-third to one-half.

For early discharge to be practical, according to this study, certain criteria must be met:

1. The patient's vital signs must be stable, with no obvious complications, surgical or medical, requiring close medical supervision in the immediate postoperative period;
2. The patient must be ambulatory;
3. The patient must be able to tolerate a normal diet;
4. Normal bowel and bladder functions must have returned;
5. The home environment must provide adequate care and supervision.

In addition, follow-up care for patients discharged early included reassuring phone calls and assurance to the patients and their families that medical assistance was readily available, as well as office visits for removal of sutures.

From the results of this study, it seems evident that patients benefit from early discharge in several ways. Exposure to antibiotic-resistant bacteria peculiar to hospitals was lessened. Patient morale was higher at home — an important factor in healing. (And financially it's a blessing to most people to go home early — hospitalization is an expensive proposition these days.)

My own experience with shortened postoperative hospitalization has been with patients who had worked with Selective Awareness Therapy enough to understand the situation and to trust themselves and their own healing powers to function effectively during the early recuperative period. Under those conditions, every surgical patient I worked with recovered much faster than would have been expected, with less pain and fewer postoperative complications.

Assisting in Your Surgery

If you are scheduled for surgery, you may be very apprehensive about it. Understanding the surgical procedure, knowing what you can expect in the hospital and after your discharge, can help you to conquer your fears. Get yourself some books from the library, and really study up on the procedure to be performed. After all, you are the person who is most concerned with your own surgery!

Since operations differ so greatly, a general exercise for postoperative healing would not be very helpful. But with what you've learned in Selective Awareness Therapy, you can create your own exercise and be comfortably and confidently in the state of Selective Awareness before you receive your pre-operative injection.

The first part of your exercise should concentrate on reassurance, to relieve any anxiety you may feel about the hospital setting and pre-operative procedures. Don't go into detail about the surgery itself — that's your doctor's job! But do review yourself waking up in the recovery room, or back in your hospital bed, feeling better than you would ever have expected possible. See yourself free of pain, comfortable and relaxed, and able to sleep normally. Review every step of the process of healing, the tissues mending quickly and cleanly, without complications.

And finally see yourself, ready to be discharged from the hospital, well on the way to complete recovery. See yourself telling a prospective patient how you prepared for surgery, shortened your hospital stay, and saved money.

Fifteen

Putting It All Together

The following case history of Karl, a young Czechoslovakian-American doctor, is included because it demonstrates so many of the points and techniques discussed in this book. As you read the tape transcript, mentally identify the factors that went into this session. This exercise will help you in your own continuing Selective Awareness Therapy.

I met with Karl only twice, to help him with the basic tools and techniques of Selective Awareness Therapy; after that, he made his own tapes and continued his therapy on his own, whenever the need arose.

Karl had no physical complaints except those associated with anxiety — when he felt pressure to perform, as in a testing situation, he would begin to tremble and sweat, he would gulp for air, and his heart would beat so fast that he thought he was going to pass out. In the state of Selective Awareness, he was able to orient back to several symptom-producing events in his childhood and to eliminate their influence on his adult life. His acute fear of failure, of being a "laughing stock" to his family and peers, caused him to become a nervous wreck whenever he was faced with a challenging situation. For example, he had failed his specialty board examinations in internal medicine three times. It was obvious that he had the training, background, and intelligence to perform at a high level; only his fear of failure stood in his way.

Karl was the youngest son in a family of refugees who had come to America when he was eighteen years old. He had grown up in a small village in Czechoslovakia, where his father was a master shoemaker; his oldest brother was a teacher, and the middle brother, following in his father's footsteps, was also a shoemaker. When, at an early age, Karl announced his desire to be a doctor, only his mother supported his ambition. His father said, "Why don't you want to be a master shoemaker like me? Do you think you're better than the rest of us?"

Whenever Karl, as a young man, passed the family shop, his father and brother would laugh at him, calling out, "Why can't you be like Arnis (the middle brother)? You'll never make a doctor!"

Another time the oldest brother, acting as a substitute teacher for the class in which Karl was a student, ridiculed him in front of his schoolmates, saying, "You'll never make it as a doctor." The father often praised both of the oldest sons, but only ridiculed the efforts of the youngest.

Following his work in Selective Awareness, Karl did pass his specialty board examination in internal medicine, which he had previously failed three times. He now has quite a successful practice and often uses Selective Awareness Therapy with his own patients.

The following tape transcript is of the second session with Karl; in the first session, he had learned how to go into the state of Selective Awareness, how to use the system of consider, consult, and consent along with the ideomotor finger signals.

Karl's Story

DOCTOR MUTKE: Take a deep breath and as you let your breath out, close your eyes, with the intention of doing nothing other than letting yourself be completely and totally relaxed. Open your eyes again, and look up toward your eyebrows. Keep looking up as you take another breath; as you let your breath out, close your eyes. Now, with your eyes closed, let your mind tune in to a scene that is totally removed from problem-solving — something that you enjoy, something that is relaxing.

When you have that scene in your mind, take another deep breath and as you let it out give yourself the suggestion, "Now relax." Let that be a suggestion toward complete and total letting go of all the muscles in your body from the top of your head to the tips of your toes. Let your forehead relax, your eyes and your eyebrows, let that feeling of relaxation go into your cheeks and your jaw until your teeth just barely touch. And feel that relaxation moving down to your neck, throat, and shoulders. Let that feeling of muscular relaxation move down to your arms, forearms, and fingers, drifting deeper and deeper with each breath. And with each breath, let your chest relax, your abdomen, your hips, drifting deeper and deeper, your thighs, your calves, the soles of your feet, and your toes, until you have the feeling that your whole body is covered with a thick, comfortable blanket of relaxation, drifting deeper and deeper. Remember that deeper means becoming more involved with your own internal state. Now, counting back from ten to zero, let every number take you deeper and deeper into awareness of yourself.

Ten — drifting deeper and deeper.

Nine — all your muscles limp and loose and relaxed.

Eight — notice how comfortable you are.

Seven — drifting deeper and deeper.

Six, five — way down deep.

Four, three, two — totally relaxed.

One, and zero.

Now pretend that your eyes are closed tightly, so tightly that you can't open them. Test your imagination, making sure that your eyes don't want to open. As you do that, notice how that action serves not only to let you go deeper and deeper and become more and more relaxed, but that it can also serve to chase away thoughts that are unnecessary and unwanted. Every time a thought pops into your mind that you don't want there, simply pretend that you can't open your eyes and you'll find that this will be very effective in blanking your mind of unwanted thoughts so that you can concentrate on what you set out to do.

When you are comfortable and relaxed and deeply aware of your internal state, allow your "Yes" finger to signal. You'll find that when your finger signals, this affirmation will serve to take you even further, deeper and deeper, to become even more relaxed.

And now imagine that you have an opportunity to talk to yourself, to review anything internal in terms of a value judgment that might interfere with your ability to take that exam. Has anything ever happened to you in terms of assuming a value judgment that has escaped your conscious attention, that may keep you from performing effectively? If so, let your "Yes" finger move; as that finger moves, you will be able to tune in, to listen to whatever comes into your mind, and to go ahead and talk about it. You will find that your own voice will serve to let you become more relaxed, to let you drift deeper and deeper.

You can learn something that gives you a better feeling about yourself. Perhaps you will orient back to an early period in your childhood, when you became sensitized and insecure, with a fear of performing well when somebody asks you a question. Orient back to a time when something happened to you like that. When you are there, let your "Yes" finger move.

KARL: ["Yes" finger signals.]

DOCTOR MUTKE: Is that the first time you knew what it feels like to be insecure? Did anything happen before that time that makes you sensitive, insecure about displaying your knowledge? Would it be all right to talk about it?

K: ["Yes" finger signals.] My father always encourages my older brothers, he never gives me any help at all, only a hard time. Only my mother tells me I'll make a good doctor.

M: Was anything ever said or done that implied that you would not make it? Listen to your internal mind. When something comes up, let that internal language give you a finger signal. Did something happen at a time earlier in your life that convinced you that you were not a good student, that you wouldn't make it as a doctor?

K: ["Yes" finger signals.]

M: What's going on? Where are you?

K: You'll never amount to anything. Become a shoemaker. [Brief silence.] Become a shoemaker — what does that mean to a kid who wants to go to school to become a doctor? Just because my father said "You are wasting your time," I think, "Don't do anything; you aren't going to make it anyway." He always measures me against my brothers, and so do I, and they always do what he wants.

M: Now go back to an even earlier time, when you were very young, and you had that feeling of, "I'm not going to make it." When you're there, in touch with that feeling, let your "Yes" finger signal.

K: I'm always behind my brothers in school, and I'm smaller because I'm younger, but I'm always comparing myself with them. And then I feel like I'm no good, because they can do things I can't. And it always seems like they know a lot more than I do, they're always picking on me about something. That's the way everybody in my family feels about me. Except my mother.

M: Now let your inner mind continue to review your childhood experiences. Counting back from ten to one, review anything relevant to insecurity, to feeling not worthwhile. [Counts from ten to one.]

K: ["Yes" finger signals.]

M: What does your review tell you?

K: There are a lot of different incidents, but it all comes down to the same thing. My father likes my older brothers better than me, because they do what he says. They're always criticizing me — "He is not going to make it anyway so why is he still going to school?" And partly I believe that I'm no good and I'm not going to make it, to be a doctor. But I want it so much, I don't care what they say! I think — maybe they're jealous, and that's why they're so hard on me?

M: Yes.

K: I feel like I'm torn between two realities — I know what I'm doing, I know I can do it; but at the same time I feel, I can't do this, I'll never make it.

M: It sounds like a situation where you would lose automatically all the time, and you can't really tell why, because you *know* you can do it.

Now relax again into your fantasy, even deeper into your own awareness. When you know that your fantasy can take over again, let your "Yes" finger show it.

K: ["Yes" finger signals.]

M: Now you are going to allow your mind to review all these events again from the viewpoint of an adult so you can reform your assumptions and set them in reality where they belong — namely, that you know what you are doing, that there is no need to let these earlier doubts interfere with your performance now.

Let your mind orient back, and when you're there, at a specific incident, let your "Yes" finger signal.

K: ["Yes" finger signals.]

M: Where are you? What are you doing?

K: I'm on my way to school, I'm in high school. As I pass my father's shop, he says in a loud voice to my brother Arnis, "There he is, on his way to school again. Sixteen years old and still in school! One of these days he'll realize he'll never make it as a doctor, and what will he do then? He's too good to be a shoemaker."

M: Would it be all right to let go of the negative influence of your father's remarks? To throw all that negative influence in the garbage pail?

K: ["Yes" finger signals.]

M: OK, now mentally construct a garbage pail, a big one with a tight-fitting lid, and just throw all the negative parts of that scene in there so it will no longer be able to influence the way you act and think and feel today. When that's done, let your "Yes" finger signal the fact that you're free of that incident.

K: ["Yes" finger signals.]

M: Now let your mind orient back to another scene. Where are you? What are you doing?

K: We're at home, we're all sitting around the table at dinner. My father is praising my brother Arnis, he's telling my mother, "This boy learns so fast, he'll be a master shoemaker by the time he's twenty." He doesn't say anything about me, but I feel worthless by comparison.

M: Would it be OK to throw that assumption of worthlessness into the garbage pail?

K: ["Yes" finger signals.]

M: Every time you do that, every time you throw a negative assumption into the garbage pail and your "Yes" finger signals, notice how free you feel, free of all the assumptions about your abilities that you've gotten from so many other people.

K: I can hear my father saying so many times, "Why don't you become a shoemaker, you aren't going to make it as anything else!" But I can hear my mother encouraging me, too, she's saying, "Don't listen to them, Karl, you're going to be a great doctor some day."

M: Would it be all right to throw your father's value judgment of you, and the negative assumptions that you have formed, in that same garbage pail?

K: ["Yes" finger signals.]

M: As you do that, notice how good it feels to get rid of all that baggage you have been carrying around. Now, whenever you're ready, let your mind return to the review.

K: ["Yes" finger signals.]

M: Where are you?

K: I'm in school, in class. My older brother is the substitute teacher. He calls on me in class, a simple question, but I just freeze up. I can't remember, I can't get the answer. In front of the whole class, all my schoolmates, he says, "You can't even answer a simple question like that. How do you ever expect to be a doctor?"

M: That's your brother's assumption, that you're not a good student. Do you need to keep that assumption, make it part of your reality?

K: ["No" finger signals.]

M: Would it be all right to let the impact of your brother's value judgment go right into the garbage can?

K: ["Yes" finger signals.]

M: OK, now continue to review your early life, and every time you come to an incident or experience or situation that reinforced a negative assumption about yourself and your abilities, consult with your inner mind — would it be all right to give that up? When your "Yes" finger signals, just throw whatever it is right into the garbage pail. You may have to construct several more garbage pails, in fact, to hold everything you want to get rid of.

Every time your "Yes" finger signals that you have thrown out another negative assumption or feeling, allow it to be replaced by the positive knowledge that you *have* made it, that you *are* a doctor, and let your confidence in your own abilities increase. Let that affirmation give you a feeling of freedom, well-being, and security. You're making room for those positive feelings by getting rid of all the garbage of insecurity and all those negative assumptions.

K: [Silence for twelve minutes, with literally dozens of affirming finger signals.]

M: Is that it? Is your review finished, all that negative stuff in the garbage cans?

K: ["Yes" finger signals.]

M: Good. Now take a deep breath, inhaling not only oxygen but inhaling life and energy as well. Think of exhaling as getting rid of not only carbon dioxide but of tension and insecurity, anything that is unneeded and unwanted, so that breathing becomes symbolic of an ever-increasing sense of security and comfort. Breathe all the way down into your abdomen. Every time you breathe, you will find that the old feelings of fear and anxiety and insecurity will make room for an ever-increasing sense of comfort; knowing that you are indeed a good student and a good doctor.

Now see yourself as you would like to be in any environment, and especially in any testing situation, secure, free of all the negative assumptions about yourself. When you have that picture in your mind, let your "Yes" finger lift. As you count from one to five and return to the state of Social Awareness, maintain that feeling of confidence, freedom, and security.

Karl's problems with achievement and his difficulty in testing situations were largely due to a classic case of sibling rivalry, made worse by a father who apparently took his brothers' sides in every situation. This meant that even when he *did* succeed, a part of himself, the part still aligned with his family, still trying to please his father, could not accept success. When he became anxious, about taking a test for example, a portion of his cortical response would actually be blocked by a biochemical reaction, and he would have no access to information that he knew perfectly well — he literally couldn't remember the answers, especially in verbal tests. When fear and anxiety took over, he would tremble and sweat, and his heartbeat and respiration would rise until he thought he was going to pass out. Obviously, his motivation was very strong, or he would never have made it through medical school.

In working out his problems through Selective Awareness Therapy, Karl did not need to relive any of his symptom-producing events, but only to review them. He was calm throughout the entire session, and he concentrated on getting at the relevant material without becoming sidetracked into analysis of other issues. His relationship with his mother, for example, was obviously important and influential in his early life, but not particularly relevant to tracking down and getting rid of the negative influences that were the target of this session.

Karl's next task in Selective Awareness Therapy, which he continued on his own, was to write down all of his achievements and accomplishments in medical school, internship, and residency. He used this list to make a confidence-building tape for himself. He also used Selective Awareness to study and review for his board examinations in internal medicine, and to practice image rehearsal of the actual testing situation.

When he took his board examination six weeks later, Karl passed in the top quarter of all those who took the test statewide. And his score was especially high on the oral portion of the exam!

Bibliography

Alexander, F., and S. A. Portis, "A psychosomatic study of hypoglycemic fatigue," *Psychosom. Med.*, 1944, **6**, 191-206.

Ax, A., and E. Luby, "Autonomic responses to sleep deprivation," *Arch. Gen. Psychiat.*, 1961, **4**, 55-59.

Barber, T. X., "Experimental controls and the phenomena of "hypnosis": a critique of hypnosis research methodology," *J. Nerv. Ment. Dis.*, 1962, **134**, 493-505.

Bard, P., "A diencephalic mechanism for the expression of rage with special reference to the sympathetic nervous system," *Am. J. Physiol.*, 1928, **84**, 490-515.

Bard, P., *Central Nervous Mechanisms for the Expression of Anger in Animals, in Feelings and Emotions*, Reymert, M. L., ed., New York: McGraw-Hill, 1950.

Bargmann, W., *Das Zwischernihirn-Hypophysen System*. Berlin: Springer, 1954.

Beam, J. C., "Serial learning and conditioning under real-life stress," *J. Abnorm. & Social Psychol.*, 1955, **51**, 543-551.

Blalock, A., and S. E. Levy, "Studies on the etiology of renal hypertension," *Ann. Surg.*, 1937, **106**, 826-847.

Bois, J. Samuel, *The Art of Awareness*. Dubuque, Iowa: W. C. Brown Co., 1966.

Brady, J. V., and F. Hunt, "An experimental approach to the analysis of emotional behavior," *J. Psychol.*, 1955, **40**, 313-324.

Broser, F., *Die cerebralen vegetativen Anfalle*. Berlin: Springer, 1958.

Bruner, J. S., and L. Postman, "Emotional selectivity in perception and reaction," *J. Pers.*, 1947, **16**, 69-77.

Cannon, W. B., *Bodily Changes in Pain, Hunger, Fear and Rage*, 2nd ed. New York: Appleton, 1929.

Cannon, W. B., "Voodoo death," *Psychosom. Med.*, 1957, **19**, 182- 190.

Cheek, D. B., "Removal of subconscious resistance to hypnosis using ideomotor questioning techniques," *Amer. J. Clin. Hyp.*, 1960, **3**, 103-107.

Cole, J. O., and R. W. Gerard, eds., *Psychopharmacology.* Washington, D.C.: Nat. Acad. Sciences, 1959.

Darrow, C. W., and E. Gellhorn, "The effects of adrenaline on the reflex excitability of the autonomic nervous system," *Am. J. Physiol.*, 1939, **127**, 243-251.

Davis, D. R., "The psychologist and experimental stress in man," in *The Nature of Stress Disorder.* Springfield, Ill.: Thomas, 1959.

Dunbar, H. F., *Emotions and Bodily Changes*, 4th ed. New York: Columbia University Press, 1954.

Erickson, Milton, "Hypnotic investigation of psychosomatic phenomena: Psychosomatic interrelationships studied by experimental hypnosis," *Psychosom. Med.*, 1943, **5(1)**, 51.

Funkenstein, D. H., "The physiology of fear and anger," *Sci. Am.*, 1955, **192**, 74.

Ganong, W. F., *Discussion in the Physiology of Emotions*, A. Simon et al., eds. Springfield, Ill.: Thomas, 1961.

Gellhorn, E., *Autonomic Regulations.* New York: Interscience, 1943.

Gellhorn, E., "Recent contributions to the physiology of the emotions," *Psychiat. Research Repts.*, 1960, **12**, 209-223.

Grahan, D. T., "Cutaneous vascular reactions in Raynoud's disease and in states of hostility, anxiety, and depression," *Psychosom. Med.*, 1955, **17**, 200-207.

Grimson, K., "Role of the sympathetic nervous system in experimental neurogenic hypertension," *Proc. Soc. Exper. Biol. & Med.*, 1940, **44**: 219-221.

Heller, H., ed., *The Neurohypophysis.* London: Butterworth, 1957.

Herrick, C. J., *The Evolution of Human Nature.* Austin: University of Texas Press, 1956.

Hess, W. R., *Die Regulierung des Blutkreislaufes.* Leipzig: Thieme, 1930.

Hinckel et al. in Silverman, Samuel, *Psychological Aspects of Physical Symptoms.* New York: Jason Aronson Inc., 1974.

Holmes and Wolfe in Silverman, Samuel, *Psychological Aspects of Physical Symptoms.* New York: Jason Aronson Inc., 1974.

Ingram, W. R., "Brainstem mechanisms in behavior," *EEG Clin. Neurophysiol.*, 1952, 4: 397-406.

Korjibsky, Alfred, *Science and Sanity*. Clinton, Mass.: Colonial Press, 1958.

Kretschmer, E., *Korperbau und Charakter*. Berlin: Springer, 1955.

Lidz and Whitehorn in Silverman, Samuel, *Psychological Aspects of Physical Symptoms*. New York: Jason Aronson Inc., 1974.

Lofving, B., and S. Mellander, "Some aspects of the basal tone of the blood vessels," *Acta Physiol. Scandinav.*, 1956, **37**, 134- 141.

Lowen, Alexander, *Physical Dynamics of Character Structure*. New York: Grune & Stratton, 1958.

Luby, E. D., C. E. Frohman, J. L. Grisell, J. E. Lenzo, and J. S. Gottlieb, "Sleep deprivation: effects on behavior, thinking, motor performance, and biological energy transfer systems," *Psychosom. Med.*, 1960, **22**, 182-192.

Marcus, H., and E. Sahlgren, "Untersuchungen uber die einwirkung der hypnofischen suggestion auf die funktion des vegetative systems," *Manchen. Med. Wchnschr.*, 1925, **72**, 381.

Mutke, Peter H. C., "Increased reading comprehension through hypnosis," *Amer. J. Clin. Hypn.*, **11**.

Mutke, Peter H. C., "Treatment of delayed breast development through hypnotherapy," presented to the Department of Neuropsychiatry, University of California, Los Angeles, February 28, 1971.

Ostrander, S., and L. Schroeder, *Psychic Discoveries Behind the Iron Curtain*. Englewood Cliffs, N.J.: Prentice-Hall, 1970.

Pavlov, I. P., *Lectures on Conditioned Reflexes*. New York: Internat. Publ., 1928.

Perls, Frederick, Rolf Hefferline, and Paul Goodman, *Gestalt Therapy*. New York: Dell, 1951.

Rogers, Carl, *Person to Person: The Problem of Being Human*. Lafayette, California: Real People Press, 1967.

Schilder, Paul, *The Image and Appearance of the Human Body*. New York: International Universities Press, 1950.

Schlosberg, H. "Three dimensions of emotion," *Psychol. Rev.*, 1954, **61**, 81-88.

Schroeder, H. A., "Pathogenesis of hypertension," *Am. J. Med.*, 1951, **10**:189-209.

Sherrington, C. S., *The Integrative Action of the Nervous System.* New Haven, Conn.: Yale University Press, 1906.

Silverman, A. J., S. I. Cohen, B. M. Shmavonian, and N. Kirshner, "Catecholamines in psychophysiologic studies," *Recent. Adv. Biol. Psychiat.*, 1961, **3**, 104-118.

Silverman, Samuel, *Psychological Aspects of Physical Symptoms.* New York: Jason Aronson Inc. (Originally published in 1968 by Appleton-Century-Crofts for Merck Sharpe & Dome.)

Stevenson, I. P., and H. G. Wolfe, "Life situations, emotions, and bronchial mucus," *Psychosom. Med.*, 1949, **11**, 223-227.

Stockard, C. R., *The Physical Basis of Personality.* New York: Norton, 1931.

Walsh, E. G., *Physiology of the Nervous System.* London: Longmans, 1957.

Wolberg, L. R., "Hypnotic experiments in psychosomatic medicine," *Psychosom. Med.*, 1947, **9**, 337.

Wolberg, L. R. *Hypnoanalysis.* New York: Grune & Stratton, 1946.

Wolfe, S., P. S. Cardon, E. M. Shepard, and H. G. Wolff, *Life Stress and Essential Hypertension.* Baltimore, Maryland: Williams and Wilkins, 1955.

TRAINING VIDEOS *From* GIL BOYNE

All Videos Available in NTSC or PAL

HYPNOTISM TRAINING

STAGE HYPNOSIS

PART ONE: GIL BOYNE – From 1960 to 1965, Gil Boyne entertained thousands with his "Hilarious Hypnosis" Stage Show in nightclubs throughout the USA This video tape combines one full hour of highly-skilled stage hypnosis techniques with the hilarious antics of a stage full of subjects.

PART TWO: ORMOND MCGILL -- Ormond McGill, Dean of American Hypnotists, presents a fascinating and mirth provoking one-hour show in his unique style. This is your opportunity to compare and learn from the art of two of the world's great stage hypnotists.   *2 hours • $75.00*

> **Bonus Offer!!**
> STAGE HYPNOSIS video PLUS Ormond McGill's book, *THE NEW ENCYCLOPEDIA OF STAGE HYPNOTISM* ($55.00 • HB • 609 pp.) for **$120.00 !!**

HYPNOTIZING DIFFICULT SUBJECTS
OVERCOMING "I CAN'T BE HYPNOTIZED"

PART ONE: DAMIEN (MISUNDERSTANDS TRANCE) -- A 22-year-old male college student has had seven sessions with two different hypnotherapists and reports he has never "been in a trance." Intake interview, instant standing induction, eye catalepsy, arm catalepsy, arm levitation, heavy left arm, handclasp response plus self-hypnosis training session. In posthypnotic interview, Damien reports he is convinced he was in a trance.

PART TWO: BOB (FEAR OF FAILURE) -- Bob, a 72-year-old Hypnotherapist, has been unable to experience trance in spite of his many efforts to do so. Using age regression, Boyne uncovers mother's

early script: "You'll never amount to anything". Bob enters into a deep trance complete with several tests. Boyne then teaches him self-hypnosis and he comes up from the trance amazed and radiant.
1 hour, 33 minutes • $75.00

INSTANTANEOUS INDUCTIONS (STANDING)

PART ONE: TWO SUBJECTS – Total Loss of Equilibrium · Eye Catalepsy · Arm Catalepsy · Deepening by Compounding · Non-Verbal Reinduction · Waking Hypnosis Creating Partial Amnesia · Creating Total Posthypnotic Amnesia · Induced Speech Inhibition · Second Instantaneous Induction · Eye Catalepsy Test · Rule of Reverse Mental Effort · Teaching Self-Hypnosis to Subject · Healing Suggestions.

PART TWO: COLIN -- A student from England has never been hypnotized before. Gil Boyne demonstrates Instantaneous Induction (standing) · Deepening by Disorientation · Deepening by Realization · Rule of Reverse Mental Effort · Deepening by Rocking Subject · Arm Catalepsy · Automatic Motion · Deepening by Pyramiding · Handclasp Response · Creating Somnam-bulism · Creating Posthypnotic Proof-of-Trance · Conditioning for Posthypnotic Reinduction by Repeated Instant Inductions · Posthypnotic Talk · Posthypnotic Reinduction · Trance Termination.

PART THREE: MOLLY (SEATED INDUCTIONS) Includes: Hand Pressure Induction · Gazing-at-the-Moon Induction · Trance Termination · Arm Levitation (Eye Catalepsy and Heavy Left Arm) · Two-Finger Induction · Clearing the Mind · Reversed Handclasp Induction.   ** *Fully Annotated !* **
1 hour, 47 minutes • $75.00

Westwood Publishing Co. • 700 S. Central Ave. • Glendale, CA 91204

HYPNOTISM TRAINING FILM #501
GIL BOYNE TEACHING AND DEMONSTRATING

Hypnotherapist, Gil Boyne demonstrates five methods of Instantaneous Induction and simultaneously explains the processes in non-technical language as he works with ten subjects. Vivid examples of Testing and Deepening, Training the Client, Developing Rapid Rapport and Re-Educating the Client using students in attendance. Includes Arm Levitation · Eye Catalepsy · Arm Catalepsy · Automatic Motion · Key-Word Reinduction · Ten Methods of Deepening the Trance Posthypnotic Suggestions · Amnesia and other hypnotic phenomena   *1 hour, 45 minutes*

Special Offer - Our best-selling video at a special price: $37.50! Includes a complete word-for-word transcript of the video absolutely *FREE!*

HYPNOTISM TRAINING FILM #300
PART ONE: ADVANCED HYPNOTIC TRAINING --

Actual live, unrehearsed demonstrations filmed in a classroom setting using the students in attendance. Gil Boyne teaches and demonstrates instantaneous inductions, testing and deepening, training the client, developing rapid rapport, and re-educating the client. PART TWO: HOW TO VISUALIZE A frustrating problem for hypnotherapists is the number of clients who report they are unable to visualize or use visual imagery. Here is how you can finally overcome that problem—forever. At a training seminar, a student informs Gil Boyne that he is unable to visualize. Watch as Boyne hypnotizes the subject and creates a process in which the subject "sees, hears, tastes, feels and smells. "   *1 hour, 45 minutes* • *$49.95*

TRANSFORMING THERAPY:™
A NEW APPROACH TO HYPNOTHERAPY
by GIL BOYNE

LEE
THE SAN DIEGO STUTTERER

In a dramatic two-hour hypnotherapy session using age regression and "uncovering techniques" Gil Boyne unveils the "battered child" syndrome and fear of castration as an initial sensitizing event for a life-long pattern of stuttering. Three years later, Lee remains totally free of stuttering. Gestalt dialogues, bodywork techniques and Parts therapy.
1 hour, 33 minutes • *$75.00*

BUNNY
PHYSICAL PAIN FROM EARLY SEXUAL ABUSE

Boyne demonstrates instantaneous inductions with several subjects. While testing one of them by making her upraised arm rigid she exclaims, "It's a miracle!" She explains that she has been unable to lift her arm higher than her shoulder for over two years. In an exciting and highly dramatic age regression Boyne discovers the cause of her arm, neck, and shoulder problems to be a result of early sexual abuse by her alcoholic father. Using several original and unorthodox techniques, Boyne creates a complete release from these disabling symptoms. Includes one-year follow-up.
1 hour, 22 minutes • *$75.00*

TED
LAW STUDENT EXAM ANXIETY

Ted is a highly-intelligent young married man, who is about to take his final exam to graduate from law school. The exam is critical because if he flunks he cannot continue his studies at the school. Intake interview fails to reveal any indications of subconscious "scripts" at work. Gil Boyne's Power Programming is used as well as self-hypnosis instruction and the daily use of hypnosis tape at home is prescribed. In a follow-up session Ted reports his amazement at his calm and efficient behavior during the exam and his almost total recall. Further programming to prepare Ted for the Calif. bar examination. Follow-up report shows Ted reporting his successful passage of the bar exam.
2 hours, 18 minutes • *$95.00*

FEAR OF CRITICISM & CURSE OF PERFECTIONISM

Gil Boyne's lecturing teaches the crippling effects of the fear of criticism and curse of perfectionism. He works with two subjects (Miriam and Sam); and discovers "childhood scripts" including the compulsive people-pleaser who "Won't say no."
53 minutes $49.95

Westwood Publishing Co. • 700 S. Central Ave. • Glendale, CA 91204

MARY
THE CHRISTMAS TREE ANGEL AND THE DEVIL
Mary learned as a child that it's "nasty" to feel good. Regression uncovers the discovery of "good feelings" in the genitals. Mother warns Mary, "Nice girls don't do that." As an adult, Mary avoids sexuality through obesity and an unattractive appearance. A two-day follow-up shows Mary nicely dressed, with her hair styled and groomed. She reports a different body image and new eating patterns. *1 hour, 6 minutes · $75.00*

BUD
BORN TO LOSE
A depressed male in his mid-fifties is convinced that he is a loser in life. Suffers from alcoholism, insomnia, low self-esteem, self-isolation and negative thinking. In two one-hour sessions on consecutive days, Bud experiences an amazing personal transformation. Filmed live before a hypnotherapy class of forty-five therapists in Chicago. Shows age regression, abreaction, Gestalt dialogues and many of Gil Boyne's original uncovering/reprogramming techniques. *2 hours • $75.00*

HOLLY/PAT
PART ONE: HOLLY ("YOU SCARE ME")
A young woman in her mid-twenties breaks into tears in the first day of a Clinical Hypnotherapy course. When instructor Gil Boyne questions her she says, "You're scaring me." This seems a paradox since Boyne has not spoken directly to her in the class. He suggests that he hypnotize her to discover the background of her emotional upheaval. In minutes she is regressed to a terrifying scene with a threatening step-father. Abreaction, re-education, rescripting and closure occur in rapid succession and the projected fear of an animated authority figure is dissipated.
PART TWO: PAT (FEAR OF PUBLIC SPEAKING)
A mature, intelligent female hypnotherapy student reports a fear of public speaking. She states that she "always sounds haughty" when speaking to a group. A comprehensive intake interview fails to reveal any evidence of negative childhood experiences or identifications. Trance is induced and deepened and a highly specialized program of affirmations and visualizations is presented.
46 minutes • $75.00

APRIL
SEXUAL ABUSE
A student develops anxiety viewing case histories. Session begins with Gestalt dream work then age regression reveals sexual abuse. April developed belief that her genitals were "dirty" and this idea developed into a recurring theme that she was bad and "dirty." April contacts her repressed anger and rage and cathartic ventilation occurs. The use of Transforming Therapy™ techniques creates a willingness to begin a process of forgiving others and herself as well. This demonstrates that the sexual abuse client can recover self-esteem without having to physically or verbally assault the perpetrator. Client has no further need to continue being the "victim" or to demand retribution.
55 minutes • $75.00

KRISTEN
WEIGHT CONTROL AND CAREER MOTIVATION
A 27-year-old former "Miss Los Angeles" complains to Boyne that her inability to control her weight has greatly complicated her life and compromised her acting career. Boyne quickly identifies an intense fear of criticism and fear of rejection, and Kristen discovers how she uses her excess weight as a protective mechanism against her own sexuality and an avoidance of taking the necessary steps to enter into an acting career (i.e., "I can't begin as long as I'm overweight.").

In three sessions of Transforming Therapy Boyne uses age regressions, Gestalt dialogues, "Saying Goodbye" and a unique form of suggestion programming. Kristen realizes the powerful subconscious impact of her mother's negative suggestions and her jealous boyfriend's angry statement, "You'll have to sleep with many men to become a successful actress." These suggestions and others have crystallized into a subconscious script "All actresses are immoral whores."

As Kristen's perception of her emotion-driven behavior is changed, a new awareness of her personal responsibility in being overweight comes to her. She confidently states that she can now manage her weight, her family relationships and begin to pursue her acting career.
2 hours, 32 minutes • $95.00

Westwood Publishing Co. • 700 S. Central Ave. • Glendale, CA 91204

MARKETING YOUR HYPNOTISM SERVICES

GIL BOYNE'S
HOW TO TEACH SELF-HYPNOSIS
HOW TO HYPNOTIZE YOURSELF AND OTHERS

Since 1956, Gil Boyne has taught self-hypnosis to more than 23,000 persons in Southern California. Boyne drew from his vast background of experience to create his most exciting project--a comprehensive course on "How To Teach Self-Hypnosis" consisting of seven hours of actual teaching on video cassette.

See and hear every element in the successful teaching of self-hypnosis, skillfully demonstrated in an actual class setting.

Includes a 99-page Marketing Manual and a complete word-for-word transcript of the seven-hour video cassette.

6 hours on 4 video tapes PLUS two manuals $195.00

Also available separately:
How to Teach Self-Hypnosis
Transcipt/Training Manual and
Marketing Manual. $35.00 each
Save! By buying both for $50.00.

HYPNOSIS FOR HEALING AND PAIN CONTROL

HYPNOSIS FOR MEDICAL EMERGENCIES
by DR. DON JACOBS
USING SPONTANEOUS HYPNOSIS TO COMMUNICATE WITH THE SICK AND INJURED TO CONTROL PAIN AND ENHANCE RECOVERY

Why is it that conversation at the scene of a medical emergency can have such a critical effect on the patient? This video shows that it is because frightened or seriously injured persons spontaneously enter into a hypnotic state of consciousness that makes them acutely responsive to certain kinds of direct or indirect suggestions.

Dramatizations and graphic illustrations present guidelines, strategies and techniques for gaining rapport and for giving suggestions and directives that can remarkably help patients control their own autonomic nervous system responses. These include: · Bleeding · Immune Response · Blood Pressure · Inflammation · Respiratory Functions · Heart Rate · Burn Injury Reaction · Dermatitis · Pain Response. *50 minutes • $75.00*

"Don Jacobs' video presents proof positive that the use of appropriate words in critical situations can not only speed healing but save lives as well."
Gil Boyne, Executive Director
American Council of Hypnotist Examiners

"As this use of hypnosis is extended there will be many lives saved."
David Cheek, M.D.
Author, Clinical Hypnotherapist

"Dr. Jacobs' approach to pre-hospital care has the potential of having a great impact on treatment outcomes."
Alan V. Brunacini
Chief, Phoenix Fire Dept.

"This tape is on the cutting edge of an exciting and innovative approach to pre-hospital care."
Bennie Cooper, M.A.
Director of Emergency Medical Training
Murray State University

FREE ! FREE ! with minimum purchase of $300.00 (Price $49.95)
Hypnosis for Healing and Pain Control
This exciting video shows the use of the pain control method developed by Gil Boyne. Excerpts from three therapy sessions include: Cure of numerous warts on an eight-year-old girl • Cure of chronic migraine headaches in a 67-year-old woman • Controlling limb tremors in a client with Parkinson's Disease.

Westwood Publishing Co. • 700 S. Central Ave. • Glendale, CA 91204

THYROIDECTOMY SURGERY WITH HYPNOANESTHESIA by WM. S. KROGER, M.D.

A clinical professor at U.C.L.A. and author of *Clinical and Experimental Hypnosis* (published by J. B. Lippincott Company), Dr. Kroger demonstrates induction and deepening and creates glove anesthesia in a 27-year-old patient with thyroid disease.

In seven conditioning sessions, the patient is taught to create glove anesthesia and to transfer anesthesia to the neck. The fifth session is a rehearsal of the surgical operation complete with surgical instruments and a verbal explanation of each step to the hypnotized patient.

In the surgical amphitheater, the patient hypnotizes herself and anesthetizes her neck and the operation is filmed and explained. Dr. Kroger creates total body catalepsy to minimize bleeding. Corneal reflexes disappear in hypnosis. Patient walks immediately after surgery.

16 minutes • $29.95

DERK
Self-Hypnosis and Ear Buzz

Student from Western Australia asked for help with a buzzing sound in his ears (tinnitus). Boyne does a complete history and while Derk is in a trance, teaches him the use of "the control panel in the brain" to eliminate the buzzing. Teaches Derk self-hypnosis. After the session, Derk reports a great improvement in his control of the buzzing sound.

57 minutes • $75.00

Self-Hypnosis Motivation Cassettes

"POWER PROGRAMMING" by *Gil Boyne*, Certified Clinical Hypnotherapist

#101 Secrets of Self-Confidence
Improve your self-image and radiate self-confidence. Overcome the fear of criticism, rejection, and failure. Feel more lovable and appreciate yourself more. $9.95

#102 Concentration, Perfect Memory, and Recall
This method is the only research-validated memory system known. It requires no memorization of key words or word associations. Liberate your photographic memory with this fool-proof cure for forgetfulness. Learn to use your automatic mind-search and memory-scanning capacity. These unique methods are programmed indelibly in your subconscious mind for your permanent use. $9.95

#103 Deep Relaxation and Restful Slumber
A new way to go to sleep! This totally effective and completely safe technique enables you to shed the cares of the day and drift off within minutes after your head hits the pillow. You float into a sleep as refreshing and rejuvenating as it is deep. You feel new vitality and energy each morning, and you maintain high energy levels throughout the day. $9.95

#104 Secrets of Success
Overcome the subconscious "will to fail." Success and riches spring from a foundation of "subconscious mental expectancy," not from a high IQ, hard work, or goodness. Develop a "success and riches" expectancy to claim the enduring success and wealth that are potentially yours! $9.95

#105M Weight Control for Men
#105W Weight Control for Women
Focuses upon the mental factors in overeating. Give yourself a new inner image of your physical self. Change your eating habits by changing your appetite desires. Improve your figure easily and quickly. $9.95

#106 Secrets of Increasing Verbal Skills and Communication
Express your ideas in a way that ensures acceptance. Overcome fear and tension at the thought of having to give a speech or a report. Learn to speak with absolute confidence and perfect poise—whether to an audience of hundreds, a small group, or a single person. $9.95

#107 Dynamics of Creative Acting
Program your mind for success in your acting career. Covers auditions, rehearsing, performing, mental attitude, and self-image. Overcome "The Freeze." Learn lines quickly and easily. Express your creativity. Similar to program created for Sylvester Stallone and Lily Tomlin. $9.95

#108 Secrets of Self-Discovery
Answers the question, "Who Am I?" Overcome the identity crisis and create a powerful belief in your own abilities. Discover your real self and your true capacity for joyful living! Teaches you how to give yourself love, acceptance, and approval. $9.95

#109 Secrets of Dynamic Health, Wellness, and Vitality
Overcome fears and negative beliefs which affect your state of health. This program subconsciously develops the mental imagery, feeling tone, and mental expectancy for radiant, vibrant expression of fitness and health. $9.95

#110 Secrets of Winning Tennis
Programmed mental images and posthypnotic suggestions developed by a top-ranked tennis player now playing in professional competition. Improves your game within days. Narrated by Gil Boyne. $9.95

#112 Dynamics of Creative Writing
This programming tape was developed for the writer/producer of a famous dramatic comedy television show. This writer later claimed that the programming was an important factor in the creation of a script which won an Emmy nomination. $9.95

#114 Stop Smoking Now!
You can overcome the helpless feeling that underlies tobacco addiction. In just a short time, you become free of tobacco—permanently! Enjoy a longer, healthier, and happier life. $9.95

#115 Sexual Enrichment for Men
You have the right to sexual happiness! Intense desire, powerful function, and glowing fulfillment are the results of using this program. $9.95

#116 Sexual Enrichment for Women
A major breakthrough in sexual programming. Overcome early inhibitions on your natural sexuality. Learn the secrets of total release and complete satisfaction. Teaches you how to be all that you can be. $9.95

#117 Success Programming for the Hypnotherapist
Created exclusively for the Hypnotherapist! Instills powerful confidence in one's ability to use hypnosis creatively, and to build a successful practice. Creates vivid imagery and covers mental and emotional attitudes and function. $12.50

Power Programming cassettes are fully audible and do not employ subliminal suggestions or musical backgrounds.

SPECIAL VALUE! Choose three cassettes for $25.00 plus $4.50 shipping and handling.
Choose six cassettes for $45.00 plus $6.25 shipping and handling.

(California residents add 8% sales tax to product total.)

WESTWOOD PUBLISHING CO.
Books and audio/video products

THE HANDBOOK OF BRIEF PSYCHOTHERAPY BY HYPNOANALYSIS
By John A. Scott, Sr., Ph.D.
Soft Cover-280pp
This book presents information beyond hypnosis into the theory and practice of advanced hypnotherapy. Why people have emotional problems and the causes and procedures of treatment. How hypnoanalysis enables people to change and the theoretical and philosophical concepts that underlie the process.

SELF HYPNOSIS & OTHER MIND EXPANDING TECHNIQUES
By Charles Tebbetts Soft Cover.139pp
A practical and comprehensive guide to the use of self-hypnosis, autosuggestion, and subconscious reprogramming for self- improvement. This new, enlarged edition includes special sections on Weight Control and Stopping Smoking. A best seller.

HYPNOTHERAPY By Dave Elman
Hard Cover.336pp
Hailed as a classic in its field. Elman's major work is a forceful and dynamic presentation of hypnosis as a lightning-fast and amazingly effective tool in a wide range of therapies. A useful and practical summation of the teachings of one of the pioneers in hypnotherapy. Elman trained more physicians to use hypnosis than anyone before or since.

HYPNOSIS: The Mind/Body Connection
By Peter Mutke M.D.
Soft Cover-192pp
A step-by-step series of easily understood procedures for making contact with and between our various physical and mental parts and functions so we may gain more control over our own health. Includes pain control, accelerated healing, weight reduction and more.

THE HEALING INTELLIGENCE
By Harry Edwards Soft Cover. 189pp
Learn how your inner healing powers work and how they can be awakened. This remarkable book illuminates the hows and whys of an extraordinarily powerful force in this new age of awareness. Harry Edwards was one of the world's outstanding and most effective healers.

HYPNO-ANALYSIS By Dave Elman
6 audio cassettes + 68pp manual
These extraordinary session in hypno-analysis consist of recordings of actual live therapy sessions presented by Dave Elman to physicians and psychiatrists. It is a rare opportunity to learn from the man who taught hypnotherapy to more healing arts professionals than any other instructor. Consists of six sessions of hypno-analysis explained and analyzed by Dave Elman.

UNLOCK YOUR MIND AND BE FREE WITH HYPNOTHERAPY
By Edgar A. Barnett. M.D. Soft Cover.155pp
Written by a medical doctor who now practices exclusively as a hypnotherapist. This dramatic book "presents fascinating case studies in which hypnosis is the demonstrated key to solving emotional difficulties Includes sections on self- hypnosis, self-analysis, and age regressions.

PROFESSIONAL STAGE HYPNOTISM
By Ormond McGill. Soft Cover.203pp
A one-of-a-kind classic work, which covers all aspects of hypnotism demonstration. Includes a thorough look at all aspects of entertaining with hypnotism, including showmanship, presentations, staging, securing subjects, and dozens of thrilling routines. A wonderful vista of entertainment that can be performed for all occasions. This book prepares you with specific directions, instructions and routines whether demo in the living room for friends or on stage in a nightclub or theater.

Use Your Credit Card and Call 800-894-9766 – Visa, MC, AE
700 South Central Avenue, Glendale, CA 91204

HYPNO- VISION
By Lisette Scholl Soft Cover 197pp
The Hypno- Vision way to better eyesight is the most innovative and effective self-help approach ever. Its key element is the simple and easily mastered technique of self- hypnosis. Hypno- Vision will help you to improve your eyesight more quickly and with longer-lasting results than any other natural system can.

SEXUAL JOY Through SELF HYPNOSIS
By Dr. Daniel I. Araoz and Dr. Robert T. Bleck
Soft Cover 222pp
This remarkable book teaches you how to overcome sexual problems that can arise through no fault of your own. Through self -hypnosis you will learn to focus your thoughts and end the power of the past to inhibit the pleasure of the present. You will be able to overcome premature ejaculation and failure to reach orgasm. You will learn to increase the intensity of your sexual experiences and achieve a more complete fulfillment. You will also gain an understanding of how your past experiences may have been affecting the expression of your sexuality.
INCLUDES AUDIO CASSETTE
Cassette #115   Sexual Enrichment for Men
You have the right to sexual happiness! Intense desire, powerful function, and glowing fulfillment are the results of using this program.
OR
Cassette #116   Sexual Enrichment for Women
A breakthrough in sexual programming. Overcome inhibitions on your natural sexuality. Learn the secrets of total release & complete satisfaction.

HYPNOTISM & MEDITATION
By Ormond McGill
Soft Cover 99pp Includes Bonus Cassette
A skillful blending of self- hypnosis and meditation, this operational manual for "hypnomeditation" clearly explains workable techniques for increasing your happiness and awareness. Fifteen days with hypnomeditation will change your life!
"Hypnomeditation " audiocassette
Here are five suggestion meditation formulas on cassette that you can use as your very own! Narrated by author McGill.

FINANCIAL SUCCESS through CREATIVE MIND POWER
Originally Titled -The Science of Getting Rich
By Wallace D. Wattles Soft Cover-92pp
Includes Cassette Tape #104
This small book is a practical manual intended for men and women whose most pressing need is for money, who wish to get rich first and philosophize after. It has been responsible for the successes of thousands of Mind Power students in the half-century since it was first published.

TRANSFORMING THERAPY
A New Approach to Hypnotherapy
By Gil Boyne Hard Cover.416 pp
Here is a radically different approach to people helping. Boyne has created a unique system that speaks simply yet eloquently to the issues of filling our deepest needs and realizing our highest potentials. Boyne focuses on solving problems by stimulating the inner creative mind Includes techniques, and complete verbatim transcripts of live therapies. This book brilliantly illustrates how Boyne's methods are currently redefining the meaning and essence of hypnotherapy.
"This book is a vivid, dramatic, clinical view into the innermost recesses of clients' emotional lives. Boyne is a gifted and creative therapist who has created a highly effective approach to hypnotherapy. "
Robert F. Reid, III, Ph.D., Professor
California State University, Northridge

FREE CASSETTE WITH YOUR
PURCHASE OF **TRANSFORMING**
THERAPY
"Success Programming for the Hypnotherapist" The only motivational program created exclusively for the hypnotherapist. It instills powerful confidence in the ability to use hypnosis creatively and to build and maintain a successful practice.

HYPNOSIS AND THE LAW
By Dr. Bradley Kuhns Hard Cover.219 pp
This training manual in forensic/investigative hypnosis is an exciting addition to the literature on hypnosis. Includes proven methods for dramatically improving recall, recollection enhancement and memory refreshment of victims and witnesses; plus transcripts of hypnotic sessions in major criminal cases.
HYPNOSIS AND ACCELERATED LEARNING By Pierre Clement,
Soft Cover.135pp
A do-it-yourself tool for self-hypnosis, divided into three parts. 1) Getting acquainted with hypnosis; 2) Acquiring self-hypnosis; 3) Utilizing self-hypnosis as a powerful learning method, including strengthening of will power concentration and speed of reading.

HYPNOTISM AND MYSTICISM OF INDIA
By Ormond McGill
Hard Cover, Illustrated.203pp
Noted author and hypnotist McGill reveals how the real mysticism and magic of India is accomplished. His detailed instructions for developing the powers of Oriental hypnotism are drawn from the secret teachings of the Masters of India, where he lived and studied for several years.

IE HEALING POWER OF FAITH:
itudy of Alternative Treatment Modalities
Will Oursler Soft Cover.366pp
oughout America, groups of people are meeting for
purpose of initiating healing. Some seek healing in
irches and prayer meetings, while others take classes
earn spiritual healing methods. Adherents of spiritual
iling have very different ideas of what illness and
iling really are. Spiritual Healing systems stand in
itrast to traditional medicine and challenge it, and the
v kinds of thinking they promote are symptoms of
found changes in our society and in ourselves.

IALYTICAL HYPNOTHERAPY
E.A. Barnett. M.D. Hard Cover 495pp
nique blend of analytic and direct suggestion
hniques. Clearly written so that they may be
ierstood by both hypnotherapist and layperson alike.
: book is well researched and very effective in its
ilanation of practice. A section on case histories forms
iajor part of the work.

IE MIRACLE OF MIND POWER
Dan Custer Soft Cover.263pp
itimulating and inspirational volume full of answers as
iow and why people grow, Custer's classic book
nonstrates the potential for better health, greater
ipiness, and increased prosperity through the dynamic
ver of the mind.

'PNOSIS AND ACCELERATED LEARNING
Pierre Clement, Soft Cover.135pp
io-it-yourself tool for self-hypnosis, divided into three
ts. 1) Getting acquainted with hypnosis; 2) Acquiring
f-hypnosis; 3) Utilizing self-hypnosis as a powerful
rning method, including strengthening of will power
icentration and speed of reading.

:YOND WORDS
Paula Slater& Barbara Sinor Soft Cover-271pp
ien we attempt to describe our inner knowledge, words
im inadequate since the fullest understanding is
'ays "beyond words." Beyond Words is a brief
:yclopedia of articles on more than 120 topics with a
of reference books at the end of each topic Topics
lude "Metaphysics", "Altered States of
nsciousness", "Transformation", and "New Age".

IE NEW ENCYCLOPEDIA OF STAGE
'PNOTISM
Ormond McGill Hard Cover- 605pp
: most comprehensive work ever produced on stage
mnotism. How to design, develop and perform a
idern hypnotic show. Over a hundred different
ithods of hypnotic induction are described in detail.
ludes openings, routines, advertising, business and
al aspect. The language is clear and simple. The
iroach is practical and down-to-earth.

"CRAZY" THERAPIES
By Margaret Thaler Ph.D. & Janja Laich
Hard Cover.263pp
An expose' of many of the strange and esoteric
alternative therapies that flourish at this time, often
combined with "hypnotherapy." This is a guide that
exposes the truth about offbeat therapies and some
individuals who call themselves a hypnotherapist. It
includes a variety of case histories of people who have
experienced controversial therapies and also
distinguishes between what is good and legal and what
is not.

PROBLEM SOLVING & GOAL ACHIEVEMENT
By Virgil Hayes Soft Cover. 156 pp
Freedom is the acceptance of responsibility for the
consequences and the rewards of one's choices. When
people make decisions to conform to the inhibitions and
limitations inflicted upon them, they have given up the
freedom to be an individual. It is Hayes' intent to present
self-hypnosis to you in a unique manner.

How to Help Yourself and Those You Love STOP SMOKING
By Jim Liles, M.S.W.Soft Cover-44pp + 2 Tapes
This highly effective system does not depend on will
power. The urge to smoke is eliminated without anxiety,
withdrawal, or weight gain. Written to assist therapists
and smokers in curing the smoking habit. The
techniques of hypnosis are explained so that the smoker
can examine there behavior, understand it, and mentally
prepare to change it. Practical and enlightening. Should
be read by anyone wanting to stop smoking or seeking
to help someone else. Cassettes included – Stop
Smoking Today and Appetite Control.

VOICES FROM OTHER LIVES
By Thorwald Dethlefsenl Hard Cover- 235pp
Dethlefsen has reached beyond Freudian theory to
reveal the connection between present neuroses and
trauma to prior experiences. Through actual dialogues
between therapist and patient we bear witness to the
dramatic, sometimes terrifying revelations from other
lives. This compelling book is highly recommended as a
teaching tool for therapists who use reincarnation
regression as a form of therapy.

HYPNOTISM TRAINING COURSE #101
By Gil Boyne
Eight audio tapes in a binder plus a 98-page manual with
numerous scripts.
Fifty hours of classroom training edited down to eight
hours of vital material. You'll hear students being
hypnotized, Boyne's answers to students' questions, all
major lectures, principles, techniques, and methods.

Use Your Credit Card and Call 800-894-9766 – Visa, MC, AE
700 South Central Avenue, Glendale, CA 91204

TITLE	Quantity	Price	Total
Analytical Hypnotherapy		$32.50	
Beyond Words		$12.95	
Crazy Therapies		$23.00	
Financial Success Through Creative Mind Power		$15.95	
Handbook Of Brief Psychotherapy By Hypnoanalysis		$19.97	
How To Help Yourself & Those You Love Stop Smoking		$29.95	
Hypno-Analysis		$99.50	
Hypnosis And Accelerated Learning		$12.95	
Hypnosis And The Law		$20.00	
Hypnosis: The Mind/Body Connection		$14.95	
Hypnotherapy		$34.95	
Hypnotism & Meditation		$15.95	
Hypnotism And Mysticism Of India		$22.50	
Hypnotism Training Course #101		$99.95	
Hypno-Vision		$12.95	
Problem Solving & Goal Achievement		$9.95	
Professional Stage Hypnotism		$14.95	
Self-Hypnosis & Other Mind Expanding Techniques		$12.95	
Sexual Joy Through Self-Hypnosis Please indicate Tape #115 (men) or #116 (women)		$15.95	
The Healing Intelligence		$12.95	
The Healing Power Of Faith		$12.95	
The Miracle Of Mind Power		$12.95	
The New Encyclopedia Of Stage Hypnotism		$55.00	
Transforming Therapy		$37.50	
Unlock Your Mind & Be Free With Hypnotherapy		$12.95	
Voices From Other Lives		$12.95	
Subtotal			
Sales Tax (CA residents only add 8 %)			
Shipping & Handling (See chart at left.)			
Total			

SHIPPING & HANDLING OrderTotal

Up to $25	$25.01-$60	$60.01-$125	Over $125
Add - $4.50	Add - $6.25	Add - $8.75	FREE

For shipping & handling outside the USA, please call or fax for quote. Specify air or surface.

Your Name_____

Company Name_____

Address_____

City_____State_____Zip_____

Phone_____

Method of Payment

□ Check Payable to Westwood Publishing □ American Express □ MasterCard □ Visa

Credit Card No._____ Expiration Date_____

THANK YOU FOR YOUR ORDER

700 South Central Ave., Glendale, CA 91204   (818)242-1159